ABOUT THE BALANCED WAY

"It is difficult to reconcile paradoxes, however in his very thoughtful book, The Balanced Way, Dr. Telmesani maps out a way to walk the fine line of excellence coupled with contentment. If you are struggling with balancing success and happiness, then this is your handbook for living a fulfilled life."

—Dr. Chérie Carter-Scott, author
If Life is a Game, These are the Rules: Ten Rules for Being Human
If Success is a Game, These are the Rules: Ten Rules for a Fulfilling Life

"This is a book of distilled wisdom gleaned from a rich career and insightful interpretation of experience in several fields of human endeavor. It is certainly recommended reading for everyone seeking contentment and a balanced self confidence in dealing with the many challenges of life. It should be required reading for people who are engaged in or preparing for careers in business, management, counseling and public service."

—Yehia A. El-Ezabi,
Professor Emeritus,
The American University in Cairo

"Dr. Telmesani presents the reader with exceptional perspectives and thought provoking ideas that focus on words of infinite significance. It's Ben Franklin meets Socrates, Wayne Dyer converses with Bill Gates, and Rumi in sync with Karl Menninger in a relaxed environment. The plan makes sense. Whether you are looking for an insightful perspective on living life or a way to move boldly forward, The Balanced Way provides those opportunities and more."

—Professor Terry Orlowski
Composer

"Reading "The Balanced Way" is an enthralling and enlightening experience. In the pursuit of worldly excellence, many of us forget where true happiness stems. In a succinct and practical approach this book is a vade mecum for those wishing to restore equilibrium and meaning in both their personal and professional lives. It is an eye opener on several levels and very well done."

—Thomas Hollowell, author,
Allah's Garden: A True Story of a Forgotten War in the Sahara Desert of Morocco

*"The best and safest thing is to keep a balance in your life,
acknowledge the great powers around us and in us.
If you can do that, and live that way,
you are really a wise [person]."*

—Euripides
(480 – 405 BC)

BOOKSURGE

Copyrights © 2009 Abdullah Telmesani, PhD
All rights reserved to the author.

ISBN: 1-4392-4412-X
ISBN-13: 9781439244128
Library of Congress Control Number: 2009905456

Visit www.booksurge.com to order additional copies.

To Reem and Ali

Acknowledgements	ix
Introduction	xi

PART ONE: **DEFINING THE BALANCED WAY** — 1

1.	Our Definition of Success	3
2.	Happiness and Contentment	7
3.	Balancing the Formula of Excellence and Contentment	11
4.	The Balanced Way	13
	Road Signs on the Path	18

PART TWO: **ELEMENTS OF THE BALANCED WAY** — 21

1.	Balanced Perception of Reality	25
	Reality is a State of Mind	25
	The Power of Expectation	27
	The State of Mind of Society	32
	Road Signs on the Path	34
2.	Freedom from the Shackles of the Past	35
	Road Signs on the Path	42
3.	Dealing Positively with Problems	45
	Models of Dealing with Problems and Obstacles	45
	The Proactive Approach	46
	Road Signs on the Path	60

4.	*Adopting Balanced Attitudes*	61
	Balancing our Priorities	61
	Choosing Our Battles	63
	Opting for Constructive Dialogue	65
	Expecting Goodness from Others	67
	Escaping the Success Trap	72
	Road Signs on the Path	75
5.	*Maintaining High Ethical Standards on Personal and Professional Levels*	79
	Moral Values from Individual to Organizational Levels	79
	The Culture of Companies and Employees' Ethics	82
	Our Ethical Tool Kit	84
	Road Signs on the Path	87
6.	*Taking the Initiative*	89
	Road Signs on the Path	92

PART THREE: **TOWARDS A BALANCED WAY** — 93

1.	*The Balanced Way: An Ongoing Development Process*	95
2.	*My Path to Excellence and Contentment*	99

Appendix I: My Current and Future Positions on the Path — 103

Appendix II: My Personal Road Signs — 167

Appendix III: List of Quotations — 169

ACKNOWLEDGEMENTS

I am indebted to many people for influencing my life positively and making this book possible. My wife, Susan Chenard, has been a great support to me in the process of writing this book and has tirelessly reviewed the manuscript. I am grateful to my friend Adel Fakeih for his continued support and keen insights. My thanks and appreciation go to Prof. Yehia El-Ezabi, Prof. Raj Jain, Mrs. Lenore Smithaman, Prof. Zohair Sibaie, Mr. Ayman Albritton, Dr. Janice and Mr. Simon Samoeil, Dr. Mohammed Ikhwan, Mrs. Deta and Dr. Cary Reid, Dr. Tarek Sida, Dr. Adnan Fakeih, Dr. Hala Aljawhari, Prof. Terry Orlowski, Mr. Mohammed Kurdi, Dr. Ahmed Badraig, Mr. Douglas Vale, Prof. Franz Douskey, Ms. Milena Rydzewski, Dr. Sahar Sibaie, Dr. Shihab Al Sawi, Ms. Virginia Winslow, Dr. Fuad Dahlawi, Mr. Reginald Chenard, and Dr. Paul Chenard for their insightful review of the material in this book.

My gratitude goes to my mentors Prof. William Doebele of Harvard University and Prof. Manuel Castells of the

University of California at Berkeley, who had an important impact on my academic and professional development.

Special thanks go to Mrs. Susan Thornton for her excellent editing of the book material.

My eternal gratitude and prayers go to my mother, Magboula Ijaimi, my father, Mohammed Ali Telmesani, and to my brothers and sisters who have always been there for me.

INTRODUCTION

Do you remember how you felt when you received news about one of your major successes, whether it was academic, professional, or social, or when you achieved one of the top objectives in your life? No doubt, it was a very pleasant moment that must have given you a great deal of happiness. As you think about it, do you still experience the same level of happiness you felt then? Naturally, we cannot sustain such a high level of happiness indefinitely.

On the other hand, if academic, professional, or social achievements bring us higher levels of happiness, is achieving success or having things go our way the only source of happiness and satisfaction? Furthermore, will we lose happiness without success?

The answers to these questions are very important to each of us, since seeking success and happiness constitutes a major element in our lives. The last question, related to whether we will lose happiness if we don't achieve success, is particularly important to us today and in the future when the impact of a global economic crisis, its future ramifications, and the ever-growing need to compete make success not just a good thing to have, but also a matter of survival. Answering such questions requires reflection on our concept of success and on how to achieve it. We must also consider our notion of happiness and ways of getting more of it, whether through success or other means.

In exploring *The Balanced Way*, you will find that the first part of this book provides a theoretical framework for concepts relevant to the balanced way and its definition. This framework includes the notions of success, excellence, happiness, and contentment—the relationship between them, the way to resolving possible conflicts among them, and how to strike an optimal balance between these vital aspects of our lives.

The second part of this book explores elements of the balanced way. These elements include the balanced perception of reality, freedom from the shackles of the past, dealing positively with problems, adopting balanced attitudes, maintaining high ethical standards on personal and professional levels, and taking the initiative. I provided sections titled "Road Signs on the Path" in Part One and Part Two of the book. These "Road Signs" include questions we need to ask ourselves concerning the topics addressed, and remind us about the main points discussed.

INTRODUCTION

The third and last part of this book establishes a broad framework and provides practical steps for assessing and enhancing our progress in achieving higher levels of balance.

In supporting the premise of this book, I have used references and quotations from Western and Eastern writers, and from Islamic literature. These references and quotations pertain to notions such as balance, destiny, the perception of reality, and freedom from the pain and agonies of the past and worries about the future. This is in addition to subjects related to dealing positively with our problems, ethics, and attitudes, on both a personal level and within the business environment.

Writing this book is not intended to be an academic exercise, but rather a process of recording an ongoing growth and learning experience I began more than twenty years ago as a husband, father, educator, and manager in both the private and non-profit sectors. This process was enriched by dealing with and learning from distinguished friends, colleagues, scholars, business associates, and international institutions, and by traveling extensively between the East and the West.

The search for the path to excellence and contentment started while I was driving to work one day in 1995. During that time, I was under tremendous pressure professionally, socially, and financially, which was taking its toll on my family and me. As I was driving, I was wondering how things would be that day, and it became evident to me that it all depended on how things went at work and with my family. As I thought more about it, I found that this question applied not only to that day, but also to every day—in fact, to my whole life. As long as things went the way I wanted them to go personally, professionally, financially, and socially, I felt happy and content. This meant that my happiness, peace of mind, and my life were vulnerable to having things happen in a favorable way, which was dependent on numerous factors, many of which were out of my control. It suddenly occurred to me that my happiness and peace of mind should not be tied to such unstable conditions, especially because things do not usually go the way we want. They actually fluctuate from day to day. From there on, I started looking for ways to stabilize and ground my life.

The challenge in achieving this state of stability is that my desire to excel, my worries about the future, and my regrets about the past, will always bring me back to an unstable, worried state of mind and to its negative consequences and attitudes. The ultimate question that stayed with me was how I could have contentment and a peaceful state of mind while not giving up my search for excellence and desires for a better future. This quest led me to my search for the balanced way.

INTRODUCTION

By writing this book, I do not claim that I have achieved the ultimate state of excellence or contentment. Seeking the balanced way, however, has been one of the best things that have happened to me. I hope you enjoy sharing this growth experience with me.

PART ONE: DEFINING THE BALANCED WAY

1. Our Definition of Success

2. Happiness and Contentment

3. Balancing the Formula of Excellence and Contentment

4. The Balanced Way

PART ONE: DEFINING THE BALANCED WAY

1. Our Definition of Success

> *"No [one] ever attains very eminent success by simply doing what is required of him: it is the amount and excellence of what is over and above the required that determines the greatness of ultimate distinction."*
>
> *—Charles Kendall Adams*

SOCIETIES use generally accepted notions to judge an individual's level of success. These notions include academic, professional, financial, and social achievements. The definition of success, however, can vary from one person to another.[1] Some individuals' definitions of success are restricted to society's general definitions of success, and hence, they measure their success according to the level of admiration they receive

---

[1] Cherie Carter-Scott, PhD, *If Success is a Game, These are the Rules: Ten Rules for a Fulfilling Life*. New York: Broadway/Doubleday, 2000, 14.

from their peers. These individuals are usually very keen on maintaining the general measures society uses for evaluating an individual's level of success.

Other individuals abide by society's generally accepted notions of success, but also add their own personal measures, which include some special or unique professional, social, or spiritual objectives. This group has a higher level of balance, as they mix society's perception of success with their own personal definitions of success and achievement.

A third example is individuals whose concept of success does not include society's generally accepted measures of success. Instead, they abide by their own personal measures, whether academic, professional, social, or spiritual. This group of individuals usually has focused views or exerted efforts that would probably lead to distinction in whatever they do, despite being less balanced in terms of their disregard for social norms. This imbalance can become more severe when individuals not only refrain from sharing their society's definition of success, but also reject the society's value system.

While there can be differences among individuals in terms of their definition of success and their ways of achieving it, a common denominator exists among all successful individuals and organizations, which is the desire to excel in whatever they do. Seeking excellence requires that we are not fully satisfied with our previous levels of achievement and success, however great they may be. This attitude creates an apparent dichotomy between success and happiness, which I will address in later sections of this book.

> *"The toughest thing about success is that you've got to keep on being a success."*
>
> *—Irving Berlin*

PART ONE: DEFINING THE BALANCED WAY

2. Happiness and Contentment

"Happiness consists in being happy with what we have got and with what we haven't got."

—*Charles H. Spurgeon*

HAPPINESS is one of the most sought-after objectives of all humans, regardless of age, race, or religion. It is usually considered a notion that is so basic and obvious that very few of us sit back and think about what being happy really means. We usually associate happiness with getting things we want or having things going our way. Getting what we want and having things go our way give us pleasure and, in some cases, tremendous happiness. However, we tend to lose that level of happiness over time, which usually makes us start over and try to get other things and achieve more objectives, hoping they will give us that elusive happiness we desire.[2]

The volatility of the relationship between happiness and the possession of material or non-material gains is a result of the fact that happiness is not tied to obtaining these gains, but rather to the level of "satisfaction," we get out of obtaining them. This level of satisfaction is high when we get those possessions or when we have things go our way.

The excitement and the surge of "happiness" we get when things go our way is a great thing to have. However, relying on having things go our way as our only source of feeling good or being "happy" can lead to a volatile mental state, and possibly make us very unhappy. We may experience distress when we do not experience favorable events or conditions (happy fixes) as frequently as we need. Addiction to such "happy fixes" could even destroy our lives.[3]

A more sustainable state of "happiness," however, can be achieved by being content with ourselves, our lives, and what God has given us. The possibility of achieving this state varies from person to person. Some individuals tend to have higher levels of "acceptance" of what they have, which makes

---

[2] "I am going to let you in on a secret: You've already got everything you need to be happy." Stephen M. Pollan and Mark Levine, *It's All in Your Head* (New York: HarperCollins Publishers, 2005), 1.

[3] The absence of happy events or achievements could lead to a state where artificial happiness is created by drugs or other deadly chemicals.

them more content. Others might find it difficult to accept themselves, their lives, and what they have. The reasons for their lack of acceptance could include ideology, a negative perception of reality, being trapped in the past, or for some psychological reasons beyond the scope of this book.

Having a low level of acceptance of our life and what we have does not mean that we cannot be content. We can train ourselves to accept our lives, what we have, and what God has given us. This can enhance our state of contentment. Developing the habit of being content leads to more contentment.

> *"Content makes poor men rich;*
> *discontentment makes rich men poor."*
>
> —Benjamin Franklin

3. Balancing the Formula of Excellence and Contentment

THE above exploration of the basic notions of happiness, contentment, and success indicates that seeking excellence requires that we are not fully satisfied with what we have achieved and that we always look for higher levels of success. On the other hand, contentment requires a state of satisfaction and acceptance of ourselves, our lives, and what God has given us.

Those two seemingly contradictory conditions prompt two important questions: Can our quest for excellence and its requisite dissatisfaction with our previous achievement interfere with our acceptance of our life, and what we have—the very things that are required for achieving contentment? Can we balance these opposing requirements?

Being so consumed with seeking success to the extent that it becomes the only source of happiness, satisfaction, or way of accepting life, can indeed obscure contentment. It could actually lead to misery if success or having things go our way is not achieved regularly or when we experience failure.

On the other hand, our quest for excellence and contentment could actually be achieved simultaneously, in spite of the apparent disparity between the two notions. Weighing these two aspects against each other is key to the path to excellence and contentment and will be explored in the following section.

> *"I define joy as a sustained sense of well-being and internal peace – a connection to what matters."*
>
> —*Oprah Winfrey*

4. The Balanced Way

HOW can we balance the apparently opposing requirements of contentment and excellence? The following metaphor demonstrates how can those opposing requirements coexist and the benefits we could get if we maintained this state of mind.

In this metaphor, we will represent our quest for "excellence" by the struggle of the captain of a ship who faces turbulent waters and perilous seas on the journey to reach new ports (successes). We will also represent contentment with our lives and what God has given us, which is required for internal stability, by the life-vests and rafts that a well-prepared captain always carries.

While the captain faces various perils in the struggle to reach new ports (or successes), he feels content having the life-vests and rafts on the ship. This state of contentment provides the captain with strength and confidence. Without the life-vests and rafts on the boat, the captain would be preoccupied by fear of storms and could reach a state of despair if the ship started to sink (facing failure or not having things go in the desired way).

If the captain lost the battle with the waves and the ship was wrecked (he failed), having the life-vests and rafts on board would protect the captain from total despair and give him another chance to stay afloat and wait for rescue or even enable him to swim to the nearest coast. If the captain, after all these efforts, did not survive the disaster, having that state of contentment, internal stability, and belief would be the best possible state he could wish for in the last moments of his life. This peaceful state would not be possible in a frustrated, angry captain without any belief or peace of mind.

On the other hand, if the captain made it to the shore, (and he hopefully would),[4] this state of mind would provide the captain with sufficient energy to continue the journey by building or renting a new ship to continue the quest for new ports (successes). With such energy, confidence, and experience, the captain might end up having a better ship than the original one he had, and reach even farther ports than the ones originally sought.

---

[4] This is because "The Power of Expectation," which will be explored in a latter section, will support him.

PART ONE: DEFINING THE BALANCED WAY

A balance between the two notions of accepting our life and what God has given us and vigorously seeking excellence is an optimal state in which we can be simultaneously successful and content. Without this balanced state, we would experience one of two extremes. The first is having success (or things going our way) as our only source of contentment. This could lead us to frustration and despair when our plans do not succeed or when things do not go our way. The other extreme is to rely on the success we have achieved, lose the desire to reach new frontiers, and hence stagnate and fall into idleness, which could lead to misery and lack of happiness.

> *"We can be sure that the greatest hope for maintaining equilibrium in the face of any situation rests within ourselves."*
>
> —*Francis J. Braceland*

Reaching a state of balance between what we want and what we have has never been more urgent than it is today and in the future. The pressure of the world economic crisis and its future consequences, and fierce and ever-growing competition, turns success from a good thing to achieve to a necessity for survival. Knowing that our life and our family's well-being depend on our sustained success could make our quest for success a very daunting experience. Failure, in such a time, could lead to more than frustration or sorrow. We must strike a balance between what we want and what we have, in order to avoid disaster.

The balance between excellence and contentment is but one facet of the balances needed for the stability of our life and the world as a whole. The balance of universal forces such as gravity, air pressure, and demand and supply, for example, provides the necessary stability in the relation between the stars and the planets, and between oceans and land; maintains a suitable living environment for humans; and regulates socio-economic relations among individuals and societies.

> *"And heaven has He raised high, and He has set up the Balance. Transgress not (due) balance."*
>
> —*Qur'an 55:7-8*

Balance is also crucial for our physical and mental health. We are reminded of this need by doctors or psychiatrists every time we have a general medical checkup or when we are ill. A publication of the Mayo Clinic asserts that whether it is too much focus on work or too little, when our work life and personal life are out of balance, stress—along with its harmful effects—is the result.[5]

Following a balanced way is not merely a virtue or a good idea, but rather a basic requirement for the stability of our lives. Bringing balance to our life will greatly enrich our mind, body, and spirit.[6]

> *"So divinely is the world organized that every one of us, in our place and time, is in balance with everything else."*
>
> *—Johann Wolfgang von Goethe*

---

[5] "Work-life Balance: Ways to Restore Harmony and Reduce Stress," *Tools for Healthier Lives*, May 31, 2008. MayoClinic.com.

[6] Jack Canfield, Mark Victor Hansen, and Leslie Hewitt, *The Power of Focus: How to Hit your Business, Personal and Financial Targets with Absolute Certainty.* Deerfield Beach, FL: HCI, 2000, 116.

Road Signs on the Path[7]

- Is my definition of success based upon achieving higher levels of acceptance in my society?

- If my definition of success is only based upon society's acceptance and appreciation of my achievements, are there other personal, social, academic, professional, or spiritual achievements that could also give me personal satisfaction?

- If society's definition of success has no place in my definition of success, is this because I do not care, I know better, or I enjoy defying society's values and norms?

- Can I strike a balance between my personal notion of success and society's broadly accepted definition of success in a way that can benefit me and my society?

---

[7] Road Signs provide a list of questions we need to ask ourselves concerning the topics of the previous sections, and remind us about the main points discussed.

PART ONE: DEFINING THE BALANCED WAY

- Does dissatisfaction with my previous achievements and my strong desire to achieve higher levels of success make me vulnerable and discontented?

- Is success as I define it, or having things go my way, my only source of happiness and satisfaction?

- Do I feel miserable, frustrated, or hopeless when my efforts to achieve success face challenges?

- Do I hear, from time to time, somebody telling me "be grateful for what you have"?

- How can I enhance my feelings of contentment in a way that gives me a higher level of internal stability and protects me from despair when my efforts to achieve success face challenges?

PART TWO: ELEMENTS OF THE BALANCED WAY

1. Balanced Perception of Reality

2. Freedom from the Shackles of the Past

3. Dealing Positively with Problems

4. Adopting Balanced Attitudes

5. Maintaining High Ethical Standards on Personal and Professional Levels

6. Taking the Initiative

PART TWO: ELEMENTS OF THE BALANCED WAY

Elements of the Balanced Way

This part of the book outlines six elements crucial for approaching the balanced way towards excellence and contentment. The first two elements, "Balanced Perception of Reality" and "Freedom from the Shackles of the Past," deal with adopting a healthy state of mind that is necessary for being at peace with our past, our future, and ourselves. Such a state of mind is important for contentment, stability, and focus needed for dealing with our present and for shaping our future.

Approaching contentment must be coupled with adopting practical steps to deal with the issues and problems we face and making proper choices and decisions on the path to excellence. These subjects are explored in the third element titled "Dealing Positively with Problems" and the fourth element, "Adopting Balanced Attitudes." The fifth element of the balanced way "Maintaining High Ethical Standards on Personal and Professional Levels" deals with aspects related to our personal and professional choices. We need to have consistency between our personal and professional actions and value systems, and to have ethical tool-kits to guide us in dealing with others that will mutually benefit us as individuals, organizations, and societies. The sixth element of this part of the book "Taking the Initiative" provides a framework for a proactive approach to adopt a balanced way towards achieving excellence and contentment.

The above six elements are not meant to cover all possible aspects of the balanced way but have been instrumental in my experience with working to achieve a higher level of balance and internal stability.

PART TWO: ELEMENTS OF THE BALANCED WAY

1. Balanced Perception of Reality

> *"The greatest discovery of my generation is that a human being can alter his life by altering his attitudes of mind."*
>
> —William James

Reality is a State of Mind

Reality is another notion, like happiness, which many of us tend to take for granted. We consider it a basic and obvious notion, and we rarely give it another look or attempt to think about it. When we describe a certain "reality," we intuitively, associate it with a certain place, a particular time, specific individuals, and certain events. The perception of any "reality," however, differs from one person to another, depending on his or her state of mind and the way he or she

THE BALANCED WAY

looks at this "reality." This can be seen clearly when different individuals experience the same situation or reality but see or describe it in different ways, as in the following examples.

After attending a party, Jane described the event as follows: "I wish I had not attended this party. It was very noisy and the food was insufficient—the grilled meats and vegetables were finished before I got to them." Because of this negative experience, Jane decided never to attend such a dinner party.

On the other hand, Mary attended the same party and described it as follows: "It was a great party—very lively and pleasant. You could hear people laughing, and the food was great, especially the grilled meats and vegetables. They were so tasty that people finished them before I even got to them. It was a great opportunity for me to make several new friends and some valuable business leads."

Jane and Mary attended the same party, yet they had very different perceptions. The reality that each experienced, was perceived, described, and responded to in two different ways. These differing responses clearly indicate that our reality is shaped by the way we perceive it.

PART TWO: ELEMENTS OF THE BALANCED WAY

"Happiness, misery, and instability come from within. It is we who give life its brightness or darkness, the same way the glass pot shapes the liquid inside it."

—*Mohammad Al Ghazaly* [8]

The Power of Expectation

Psychiatrists and self-help specialists agree that looking positively at life and the future and expecting good things to happen will have a positive impact on our lives. In his book *You'll See It When You Believe It*, Dr. Wayne W. Dyer asserts that we can shape our life and get what we want if we believe we will. Rhonda Byrne, in her book *The Secret* talks about the "Law of Attraction." This law states that having a clear and confident image of what we want in the future will no doubt make it happen. Dr. Joseph Murphy argues in his book *The Power of Your Subconscious Mind* that transmitting a clear idea or a mental

---

[8] Mohammad Al Ghazaly (1917–1996) was an Egyptian cleric and scholar whose ninety-four books interpret the *Qur'an* in a modern light. He has been called one of the most revered scholars in the Muslim world. Qouted in Abdullah Telmesani, *Between Acceptance and Excellence: Concepts and Principles on the Path to Success*. Jeddah, Saudi Arabia: Almahmoudiah, 2002, 13. (In Arabic language).

picture about the future to our "subconscious mind" will turn this idea or mental picture into a reality.

Looking at these theories and at positive thinking theories in general, we see a common denominator among them, which is: the way we look at the future and our expectations of it does somehow shape the future. This common denominator seems to hold true for many people, regardless of the name of the approach or its logical explanation.[9] This leads to an important question about the power behind these and other positive thinking theories. Looking into this question, I found an answer in a Divine law, which clearly indicates that if we confidently expect good things in the future, we will get them; and if we expect bad things, we will get them.[10] This power of "expectation" is readily available to all humans, regardless of their belief. When we expect a better future (which is a facet of time) this is in itself a form of expecting good things from God.[11]

---

9 This is evident from the responses of readers of books such as *The Secret* and other books related to positive thinking, and indicated by the cases cited below.
10 "I am as My servant expects from Me; if he expects good, he gets it; and if he expects bad, he gets it," (a *Divine Islamic Tradition (Hadith Qud'si)*). Islamic *Devine Traditions* are attributed to God, narrated by Prophet Mohammed, in accordance with revelations. *Devine Tradition* is the third source of Islamic Tradition, that are: *Qur'an, Prophet Mohammed Tradition (Hadith)*, and *Divine Tradition (Hadith Qud'si)*.
11 "Don't curse time, for I am time," (a *Divine Islamic Tradition*).

PART TWO: ELEMENTS OF THE BALANCED WAY

Relying on this power does not take away from the benefits of the ideas offered by the theories mentioned above, as they are manifestations of the same law. We can use these techniques to focus on getting specific things or reaching certain targets. Limiting our wishes and expectations of the future to specific gains is not the only approach we can follow. We do not really know all the possible good things we might receive in the future, and we cannot be sure that what we have asked for is truly in our best interest in the grand scheme of things. Hence, we should also ask God to choose the best for us and for our loved ones that could be beyond the needs we currently foresee, expect, or comprehend. Let us look positively to our future, despite negative thoughts and doubts. Negative thoughts, doubts, and fears of the future create obstacles in our way towards happiness and success.

In the summer of 2001, the racecar driver Dale Earnhardt, Jr. had a severe shock after his father NASCAR legend Dale Earnhardt, Sr. died in a race accident when he hit the wall of the racetrack. Following that incident, Earnhardt, Jr. was naturally very preoccupied by his father's accident, and the danger of hitting the wall of the racetrack. In the very first car race that followed his father's accident, Earnhardt, Jr. survived an accident where he hit the wall of the track in a wreck eerily similar to his father's. Did Dale's fears of such a wreck somehow draw this experience to him?

> *"The only thing we have to fear is fear itself — nameless, unreasoning, unjustified terror which paralyses needed efforts to convert retreat into advance."*
>
> *—Franklin D. Roosevelt*

Another example of the impact of fear and expecting the worse is that of a woman who was well off but suffered the recurring fear of ending up as a bag lady on the street. In her attempts to protect herself from such a nightmare, she searched for the best investment fund she could find with the highest return and lowest risk. She deposited her life savings in Bernie Madoff funds,[12] two weeks before it was revealed that he had misappropriated his clients' funds in a global Ponzi scheme. Her fear of becoming a bag lady is now as close to reality as ever.[13]

Fear of the future, according to the "law of expectation," represents negative expectation of God's will to bring us good things in the future. Negative expectations bring negative results. Fear of the future and panic about what might happen

---

[12] Bernie Madoff pled guilty in March 2009 to eleven felonies including securities fraud, and admitted defrauding his thousands of investors. The estimate of client losses was $65 billion.

[13] This story was aired on CNN in January 2009.

PART TWO: ELEMENTS OF THE BALANCED WAY

next, seem to have a way of disrupting our future, and actually stand in the way of good things coming our way. It is difficult for good, confident, and relaxed swimmers to stay under water long enough to drown, as the "law" of buoyancy will keep pushing them up. It is equally difficult for a panicked or inexperienced swimmer who is afraid of drowning to stay afloat. The sheer fear and erratic splashing, and hence, loss of breath and water swallowing, will bring a panicked swimmer down. On the other hand, if someone with no previous swimming experience was somehow convinced, beyond doubt, that he or she would never drown, this person could lie calmly on the surface of the water with his or her arms and legs spread and would float. The swimmer's fear of drowning and its consequences negate the force of the law of buoyancy that is meant to help him or her float.

I have a close friend who was separated from his boat while scuba diving in the Red Sea. In spite of his gloomy prospects of surviving, he had no doubt in his mind that he would survive because of his complete and utter belief that God would help him for the sake of his family. He ended up staying afloat for forty hours (between 4 p.m. on Thursday and 8 a.m. Saturday), until he was picked up by coast guards outside the port of Jeddah, Saudi Arabia. At times, Hosam felt that the white-tipped reef shark following him most of the time was actually not going after him, but rather keeping him company until he reached shore safely. The power of belief and positive expectation can indeed give us infinite strength. Hosam's experience showed that power to him, to me, and to many others.[14]

Submitting our fears to God with the confidence that things will turn out for the best is within our grasp. All we must do is reinforce this belief and receive its bounties. We can even change what is written for us in destiny by asking God, with confidence, to rewrite our destiny in the way we want it to be.[15] Knowing that we can even change our destiny should give us even more confidence about our future.

The State of Mind of Society

The impact of adopting a certain state of mind, whether positive or negative, confident or desperate, is not restricted to the individual, but can affect an entire society. On an economic level, it has been proven theoretically and practically that the spread of the fear of economic recession among individuals in society can actually lead to a recession, even if

---

[14] Hosam Joma is a PhD graduate from the University of Pennsylvania (1990) and an Assistant Professor of Landscape Architecture at KAAU, Jeddah, Saudi Arabia.

[15] "Only prayers can change destiny." (a *Prophet Mohammed Tradition*).

the conditions for a recession are not fully present. The mere expectation of an economic downturn can lead to a decline in stock market prices and encourage individuals and organizations to hoard available cash, and hence, avoid buying unnecessary goods and services or entering into new investments. Lower sales then lead to a further economic decline, layoffs, and lower purchasing power, which lead to a further decline, and so forth. This state of decline can indeed lead to a real recession, unless the attitudes and expectations of individuals and organizations within society are changed. In such cases, governments take all possible measures for reinforcing confidence in their local economies. Once confidence improves, the economic decline levels off and growth restarts, even if growth conditions are not fully present.

It also holds true that when a general feeling of confidence and strength become prevalent within society, that society will eventually become stronger. Society's perception of itself and its future reflects its reality and shapes its future.

> *"Verily never will God change the condition of people until they change what's in their hearts."*
>
> —*Qur'an, 13:11*

THE BALANCED WAY

Road Signs on the Path

- Do I feel that I have a negative perception of reality?

- Do people tell me, from time to time, that the situation is not as bad as I think it is?

- Do I notice that people avoid me when I complain or when I make negative comments about myself or others?

- Knowing that my state of mind shapes my reality, how can I improve the way I look at reality?

- Do I find myself in a continuous state of fear of the future?

- Does trusting God with my life and the lives of the people I love give me a higher level of contentment and peace of mind?

- How can I improve my expectations of God's mercy and kindness?

PART TWO: ELEMENTS OF THE BALANCED WAY

2. Freedom from the Shackles of the Past

OUR past has periods of happiness and good times. It also has moments of pain, bad decisions, and lost opportunities. While feelings of happiness fade away as time goes on, moments of pain and sorrow seem to stay with us for longer periods.

Losing a dear one, missing a great opportunity, experiencing injustice, being hurt by others, or making disastrous decisions that seem to affect our whole life negatively can make us feel sorrow, frustration, or anger. We may also feel jealousy for others who seem to have it better than we do. With time, these feelings can create a heavy burden on our heart. They can drain the positive energy that we need in order to march strongly towards the future. These unhappy feelings can also manifest themselves, not only mentally, but also physically in the form of tightness in the chest, fatigue, or muscle or joint pain. We cannot easily ignore such negative feelings, and we cannot eliminate them just by knowing they affect us negatively. These feelings reside deep inside us.

Feelings of regret about what has happened, what we have done or have lost, or feeling jealous of people who we think have had it better than we, are all feelings that revolve around rejecting or not being at peace with the past. We tell ourselves "It should not or could not have happened this way if we or others had done something differently."

This state of rejection usually comes from a mix-up in our mind between the notions of "action" and "destiny." While it is important to take action in improving our lives and while we do have the ability to positively or negatively influence our lives, once something happens, it is instantly moved from our "zone of action" to the "realm of destiny," or what some of us might call a "fait accompli" or a "done deal". This "done deal" is what we must accept, for what has happened could have never been different.[16]

> *"We often ask, 'Why did you do that?'*
> *or 'Why did I act like that?'*
>
> *We do act, and yet everything we do*
> *is God's creative action.*

---

[16] "Whatever missed you was not meant to hit you, and whatever hit you was inevitable (unavoidable)," (a *Prophet Mohammed Tradition*).

PART TWO: ELEMENTS OF THE BALANCED WAY

We look back and analyze the events of our lives,
but there is another way of seeing,
a backward-and-forward-at-once vision,
that is not rationally understandable.

Only God can understand it."

—Rumi[17]

Accepting that what has happened in the past could have never been different, regardless of what we or others could have done, takes the past (and thus the responsibility for not changing it) out of our "zone of action." Reaching this level of understanding gives us a sense of relief and positive energy that will enable us to focus on what is within our zone of action. This includes learning lessons from the past to avoid repeating similar mistakes,[18] or bad deeds;[19] eliminating, as far as possible, the impact of these mistakes on ourselves and others; not allowing others to hurt us or to influence

---

[17] *The Essential Rumi.* Translated by Coleman Barks (New York: HarperOne, 2004), 26–27.

[18] "If you have made mistakes, even serious ones, there is always another chance for you. What we call failure is not the falling down, but the staying down." Mary Pickford. Quoted in Applewood Books series, *Success: Quote/Unquote,* (Bedford, Massachusetts: Applewood Books, Inc., 2002), 15.

[19] "Without doubt, I am He that forgives again and again, those who repent, believe, do right, and are ready to receive true guidance," (*Qur'an*, 20:82).

our lives negatively; making peace with and trying to forgive people who have hurt us;[20] and most importantly, forgiving ourselves.

> *"It really doesn't matter if the person who hurt you deserves to be forgiven. Forgiveness is a gift you give yourself. You have things to do and you want to move on."*
>
> —Real Live Preacher

Acceptance of whatever has happened in the past (whether good or bad) will bring us more contentment and blessings in the present and the future.[21] Forgiveness brings us freedom from the past, peace of mind, and a happier future.[22] Discontentment, hatefulness, fury, and frustration about the past lock us up in the misery of the past and block our vision of the future and its opportunities.[23]

---

20 "If one forgives and makes reconciliation, his reward is due from God: for He loveth not those who do wrong," (*Qur'an*, 42:40).

21 "Whoever is content will get contentment, and whoever is discontent (mad, furious, or rejecting) will get the same," (a *Divine Islamic Tradition*).

22 Jack Canfield, Mark Victor Hansen, and Les Hewitt, *The Power of Focus: How to Hit your Business, Personal and Financial Targets with Absolute Certainty* (Deerfield Beach, FL: HCI, 2000), 170.

23 "When you say "yes" to the "isness" of life, when you accept this moment as it is, you can feel a sense of spaciousness within you that is deeply peaceful." Eckhart Tolle, *Stillness Speaks*. Novato, California: New World Library, 2003, 67.

PART TWO: ELEMENTS OF THE BALANCED WAY

Liberating ourselves from the shackles of the past requires a profound understanding of the notions of "action" and "destiny," and finding ways to eliminate unnecessary and harmful mental and physical states. A practical and effective way to free ourselves from the negative mental and physical impact of the past is to look at feelings of sorrow, pain, jealousy, and responsibility for not changing what has already happened in the past as a load on our chest and shoulders that is not ours to carry and that should be dropped.

Freeing ourselves of this unwanted load can be accomplished by a simple breathing exercise. In this exercise, take a deep breath that slowly fills up your lungs and exhale while visualizing the pain, sorrow, and feelings of responsibility for not changing what has happened in the past coming out of your chest and off your shoulders and returning to God, the Guardian of Destiny.[24] Repeating this breathing exercise at least five times, whenever you feel any kind of sorrow or heavy load on your chest and shoulders, is (from real experience) extremely effective in alleviating those physical and mental agonies. Continuing to perform this breathing exercise whenever you feel sorrow or pain will bring you to

---

24 Believing in destiny is one of the six Pillars of Belief in Islam, which are: Believing in God; His Angels; His Holy Books (the *Torah*, the *Bible*, and *Qur'an*); His Apostles (Adam, Noah, Abraham, Moses, Jesus, and Mohammed); the Day after; and Destiny—both the good and the bad of it.

a state of total freedom from past burdens. You will experience abundant energy to deal with your reality, avoid previous mistakes, prevent others from hurting you, and move to the future with full energy and agility.

> *"Don't let your throat tighten with fear.*
> *Take sips of breath all day and night,*
> *before death closes your mouth."*
>
> —*Rumi*[25]

Neuro-linguistic programming (NLP) experts use similar visualization methods in purging thoughts of the past or reshaping that past in one's mind.[26] While NLP techniques rely on the individual's imagination in eliminating or modifying those images of the past, the exercise suggested above relies on God to relieve us of unnecessary and harmful feelings for good. Saying this does not preclude the usefulness of NLP or similar techniques. Using NLP, meditation, breathing exercises, or other techniques, while keeping the notions of "action" and "destiny" in mind, will be even more effective

---

25　*The Essential Rumi.* Translated by Coleman Barks (New York: HarperOne, 2004), 52.
26　Steve Andreas, and Charles Faulkner, eds., *NLP: The New Technology of Achievement.* New York: HarperCollins Publishers Inc., 1994, 17.

than conducting mechanical exercises without connection to a higher power.

The simple breathing exercise suggested above can also relieve us of our fears about the future. Knowing that our worries about the future will not make it better should lead us to seek God's help to get rid of them. Feeling alone with no connection to or support from a higher power exacerbates our fear of what could happen in the future, which according to the "law of expectations," will make it a reality.

Conducting the above exercise and having all our fears of the future submitted to God will lead to a state of "positive submission"—a state filled with contentment, freedom from our fears, and abundant energy. Such a state will allow us to focus on what is within our zone of action and confidently shape our future. This confidence in a better future will actually shape the future in the way we want.

> *"I have learned from experience that the greater part of our happiness or misery depends upon our dispositions, and not upon our circumstances."*
>
> —*Martha Washington*

Road Signs on the Path

- Do I experience feelings of sadness or frustration when I remember past failures and unhappy events?

- Do I regularly have the nagging feeling that painful and unhappy experiences should not have happened, or feel responsible for not changing them into something better?

- Can I reinforce my acceptance of destiny to the extent that gives me a higher level of contentment and liberates me from my feelings of sorrow, pain, anger, and responsibility for not changing what has happened in the past?

- Do I feel contented and free when I perform my deep breathing exercise or a similar technique?

- If the breathing exercise (or any similar technique) does not give me a sufficient level of contentment, is that because I do not

PART TWO: ELEMENTS OF THE BALANCED WAY

want to free myself from the past pains and agonies?

- Can I work harder to change my attitude towards the past?

- Can I benefit from my experiences in avoiding new failures?

- Do I occasionally feel frustrated and jealous of others who have achieved certain successes or acquired things I did not get?

- Do I feel that what others have received, I should have received too?

- Knowing that what others have received, whether it was good or bad, was meant to happen regardless of what they or others could have done, can I be happy about the good things that have happened to them and remember that thinking positively about what they got will bring good things to me?

PART TWO: ELEMENTS OF THE BALANCED WAY

3. Dealing Positively with Problems

> *"Unrest of spirit is a mark of life; one problem after another presents itself and in the solving of them we can find our greatest pleasure."*
>
> —Karl Menninger

Models of Dealing with Problems and Obstacles

People vary in the way they deal with problems and obstacles in their daily and professional lives. The way we deal with problems and obstacles shapes our ability to succeed in life. Three approaches for dealing with problems are outlined below:

1. The "passive": a characteristic of individuals who give up whenever faced with a problem. This approach reaches its ultimate level in the case of individuals who use their problems and

obstacles as excuses for failure or as a means of seeking sympathy from others.[27]

2. The "positive": a characteristic of individuals who do not give up when faced with problems or obstacles. They instead work hard to solve them.

3. The "proactive": a characteristic of individuals who not only work on solving the problem but also use problems as opportunities to create more success.

The Proactive Approach

We can do many things to avoid problems before they develop; however, once problems (or anything for that matter) happen, they are transformed from our "zone of action" to the "realm of destiny." This situation requires that we accept our problems as incidents that could have never been any different. This acceptance gives us feelings of serenity and

---

[27] "He that is good for making excuses is seldom good for anything else," Benjamin Franklin. Quoted in Ashton Applewhite, William R. Evans III, and Andrew Frothingham, eds., *And I Quote: The Definitive Collection of Quotes, Sayings, and Jokes for the Contemporary Speechmakers.* (New York: Thomas Dunne Books, 2003), 3.

PART TWO: ELEMENTS OF THE BALANCED WAY

stability, and allows us to focus on suitable ways of dealing with those problems. The following are several steps to help in dealing with such problems:

1. *Avoid looking at problems as "unsolvable."*

    By considering problems unsolvable, we turn them into closed boxes. We cannot see what is inside a closed box —let alone properly deal with it. If we consider a job or social problem a "total disaster that we can't do anything about," then we cannot think about proper ways for dealing with it, and hence it becomes truly "unsolvable."

2. *Dismantle the problem into smaller parts.*

    Whenever we have a big problem, we tend to combine it with all its related issues. Such an attitude makes the problem look more severe and complicated than it really is. Separating the related issues from the main problem and dealing with them individually will reduce the magnitude of the problem and its burden and help us to arrive at a better solution.

THE BALANCED WAY

> *"Nothing is particularly hard if you divide it into small jobs."*
>
> —*Ray Kroc*

The entanglement of a problem's elements and the inter-dependency of those elements with each other is, in many cases, the real problem. Dismantling the elements of the problem can sometimes reveal how simple the problem really is or even show us that we have no problem at all.

In many cases, we refrain from starting to deal with a certain element of the problem, thinking that solving that element requires dealing with or solving other elements at the same time. This approach creates a vicious cycle. It may prevent us from taking initiative in dealing with the right parts of the problem or from making any progress at all.

As will be shown in the case study at the end of this section, freeing the elements of the problem from each other as much as possible opens the way to solving them. The resolution of one part of the problem will make it easier to (or automatically) solve the other parts that depend on it.

I have repeatedly dealt with individuals who would give up on solving a problem after running into obstacles. These obstacles were usually related to assumptions they had made about the problem or elements related to it. When allowed time to look at the problem in different ways and challenge assumptions about the relationship of the components of the problem, one can always arrive at good solutions. Sometimes I hear the comment "Oh, that could do it" from someone who did not want to deal with the problem, which sounds to me like saying "If you want to look at it this way, of course, it can be done." My response would usually be "Why not?"

"Whenever I hear, 'It can't be done,' I know I'm close to success."

—Michael Flatley

Dismantling the problem and breaking it into "smaller problems" to address independently requires that we challenge assumptions about the interdependence of the elements of the problem. One way to do this is to keep asking questions about the relationships between different parts of the problem and the possibility of solving any of those elements independently.

3. *Reexamine our role in the problem.*

   It is always easier to blame others for the problems we encounter. We tend, sometimes, to avoid looking at the possibility of being the cause of the problem or at least a factor in its perpetuity. This is due either to our own bias towards ourselves or because we fail to look at the problem from all sides. Starting with the assumption that other individuals or circumstances must change so that our problems can be solved is not always best. It complicates problems that could easily be solved by simply changing ourselves.

PART TWO: ELEMENTS OF THE BALANCED WAY

An old story tells us that a king hurt his foot while walking in the street. In response, he issued a royal decree that all the kingdom's streets be covered with soft leather. Faced with such an impractical order, a wise assistant thought deeply about the problem and decided instead to cut two pieces of soft leather and fit them to the king's feet. According to this old story, this is how shoes were invented.

4. *Look at the problem in terms of its spatial and temporal dimensions.*

   Introducing some changes to the spatial aspects of the problem and looking at it through different timeframes might help in solving or reducing the impact of the problem. For example:

   a) Examine the possibility of introducing some positive changes to the geographical aspects of the problem and its related elements. This may reduce the magnitude or the impact of the problem. Such changes could include moving some of the problem elements or participants from one place to another.

b) Look at the problem in different timeframes (a year, five years, or ten years), taking into consideration the changes that take place with time, such as aging and other social and economic aspects. In many cases, it is surprising to discover the limited impact the problem will have beyond a certain time. This discovery will give us a feeling of relief and allow us to see alternative ways of dealing with the problem. We may even discover new opportunities that are associated with the problem.

"Frame every so-called disaster with these words...In five years, will this matter?"

—*Regina Brett*

PART TWO: ELEMENTS OF THE BALANCED WAY

5. ***Co-exist with problems we cannot resolve.***

    Some problems, by their nature, or for the lack of better solutions, do not go away but instead become part of our lives. When that is the case, something must be done to improve our co-existence with such problems. We must reduce their negative impact on us and on others as much as possible.

    Before exploring ways to co-exist with a problem, we have to keep in mind that we should never ever give up looking for a solution, even when it looks like none exists. By looking at the problem from time to time and applying the steps explained above (or similar techniques), we might be surprised to find that it is possible to find a solution after all.

"Many of life's failures are people who did not realize how close they were to success when they gave up."

—Thomas A. Edison

THE BALANCED WAY

We can co-exist with problems in a way that reduces their impact until we find solutions for them using the following steps:

1) Compare our problem with others we have faced (or might have faced) that could have been much worse.

2) Look for positive aspects of the problem and the lessons learned from them. Find ways to use them to avoid similar problems in the future.

3) Redefine the problem. Give it names that are more acceptable, both psychologically and socially, or apply your sense of humor. I once heard a good example of this technique. A person who had spent time in a mental institution overcame the stigma related to this experience by smiling and referring to the time he spent in the "club."

"I think the next best thing to solving a problem is finding some humor in it."

—Frank A. Clark

PART TWO: ELEMENTS OF THE BALANCED WAY

The above steps are examples of ways we can follow to deal with problems positively. Following such steps allows us to make a quantum leap from the state of helplessness, pain, and suffering in which we may find ourselves. Thus, we can reach a proactive state and deal positively with our lives. As we continue to deal with problems and develop similar attitudes, we will also improve our mental fitness. We may find that dealing with problems becomes a hobby rather than a burdensome chore.

Case Study:

This case study demonstrates the impact of following the above approach within an organizational environment. We can apply a similar approach to personal issues.

While working in a developing country, an international company faced a serious problem. Governmental officials had taken a position against the company that restricted its ability to acquire licenses to implement its real estate development projects. This position made it not possible for the company to recoup the money it had invested during the prior four years. Letters sent by governmental officials to the company clearly indicated their apathy and lack of interest in providing assistance to the company.

THE BALANCED WAY

The problem looked very complicated. For four long years, the company faced a stalemate, even after spending millions of dollars on the problem. This lack of progress and the resulting financial losses led to a decline in the morale of the company as a whole, and rising conflicts among the company's employees and executives that further damaged efficiency while raising costs.

What made the situation even worse was that the company could not solve the problem by ceasing its operations, for such a move would have made the company liable for severe legal and financial penalties. It was obliged to execute its projects after benefiting from the special facilities extended to it by the government.

In an attempt to resolve this stalemate and stop the ongoing depletion of its resources, the company recruited the author as its deputy general manager. After carefully examining the problem, the problem-solving method outlined above was applied. First, looking at the problem as "unsolvable" was avoided. Next, the elements of the problem and the nature of the relation between them were specified. Third, elements that did not have a direct influence on the continuity of the problem were separated from each other. Fourth, elements that perpetuated the impact of the problem were specified, and focus was placed on resolving them as the top priority.

Last, the company was advised of the possibility of changing itself before changing others.

As this process was followed, it became evident that many of the issues the company owners cited (while being related to the problem) had nothing to do with its continuing impact. The source of the company's problem was actually in the way it was dealing with local officials. At the beginning of its operation, when the company faced some difficulties in getting the permits to start constructing its projects, company officials had sent numerous letters to governmental offices, complaining of the company's inability to get building permits and pointing out that this inability prevented the company from implementing its investment projects. Those letters had raised doubts among government officials about the company's sincerity in implementing the projects to which it had committed itself. Government officials believed the company was using the delay of the permits as an excuse for its lack of commitment, especially after the company had benefited from the investment incentives given to it by the government. The complaint letters had also antagonized the governmental organizations that issued building permits, which further complicated the issue.

Instead of continuing to attempt to change the government officials' attitude by meeting with them, sending more letters, or even suing the permit-issuing agency, the company's new tactic was to focus on revising and insuring the completion of documents required for securing the permits. These documents were found to be outdated, due to the constant involvement of technical departments and their consultants in the disputes with governmental agencies. The process of document preparation was combined with sending indirect messages to decision makers, citing progress in processing permit documents and the company's sincerity in obtaining the permits and implementing its projects. As a result of these efforts, the company obtained the permits in less than six months.

The company's owners were pleasantly surprised that the government officials who were previously considered unsympathetic were very happy when the company obtained the permits and was ready to begin the implementation of its projects. These officials also visited the company to express appreciation of its initiatives, promised to alleviate current difficulties, and gave additional help and permits to the company to compensate for its previous losses.

The resolution of the problem and the beginning of work on the investment projects consequently raised the morale of the company, increased efficiency, minimized legal disputes, and turned the company from a struggling organization into one of the most successful foreign real estate development companies in the country.

In addition to demonstrating the impact of following the above-mentioned steps in dealing with problems and obstacles, this case study also indicates the following precepts:

1. The incorrect definition of the problem creates more problems and further delays to its solution.

2. Rigorously challenging previous assumptions is crucial to solving problems.

3. It is better to deal with some of the elements of the problem indirectly. Direct confrontation might expand the problem and could have a negative impact on progress.

4. Nobody likes complainers and people with excuses.

5. Success breeds success.

Road Signs on the Path

- Do I occasionally find myself unable to deal with my problems?

- Do I sometimes talk about my problems and my bad luck in an attempt to win others' sympathy or to justify my failures?

- Do I feel frustrated and desperate when I face problems to the extent that I am unable to deal with them?

- How can I follow the proactive approach of dealing with problems or a similar approach, towards solving them?

- If I cannot resolve some of my problems, can I at least achieve a state of coexistence with them?

4. Adopting Balanced Attitudes

Balancing Our Priorities

Our behavior, decisions, and choices reflect our priorities. Specifying practical and consistent priorities gives us a firm ground for balanced decisions and choices. If we look closely at our previous failures and the problems we face, we will find that most result from decisions and choices not based upon clear or consistent priorities. If we do not have a clear framework of balanced priorities, our actions become arbitrary and can conflict with each other. This may lead to bad results or even acute problems. We then blame bad luck or "others" for our own failures.

Being so impatient, rigid, or critical of our family members to the extent that our family life is disrupted (or having continuous conflicts with our friends or people we have to deal with) is a clear sign of a lack of balance in dealing with our priorities. Being too proud or over-sensitive to our colleagues and superiors' views of our performance or being too rigid in dealing with common work-related issues can create problems as well. These problems include repeated confrontations with colleagues and coworkers, regularly moving between jobs, and hence, undergoing continuous financial complications. Focusing on work to the extent of ignoring our families, loved ones, or our own health is also a sign of a lack of balance in our priorities. Not having clear criteria for selecting projects or initiatives to be involved in or randomly committing to projects that divert our focus from things that count in our life is a sign of a dysfunctional priority system.

Giving any aspect of our life too much value compared to others causes disruptions in our lives. This disruption not only applies to our daily life but also to our obligations towards God. Giving religious activities top priority to the extent of ignoring other aspects of our lives is also a sign of unbalanced priorities.[28] An even more acute state of such imbalance is religious fanaticism, a state associated with ignorance that further leads to an imbalance in judgment, and hence, irrational actions that could harm individuals and societies as a whole.

---

28 "Surely, there are obligations towards your Lord, other obligations towards yourself and still others towards your family, so you have to give each it's due." A statement made by Salman Al Farisi and acknowledged by Prophet Mohammed.

PART TWO: ELEMENTS OF THE BALANCED WAY

"Ruined are the fanatics [who follow extremes in matters of Faith]."

—Prophet Mohammed

Balancing our priorities requires wisdom and maturity. While it is not easy or possible to make a sudden change in our level of wisdom and maturity, the mere awareness of how important it is to specify clear and balanced priorities in our professional and social lives is in itself a quantum leap towards improving these priorities. Such balance will bring us higher levels of contentment and success, and save us from wasting our nerves, energy, and financial resources.

Choosing Our Battles

In his book *The Art of War* Sun Tzu asserts that our best battles are the ones we win without a fight. Achieving our objectives without confrontations or physical or mental losses is the best victory. We do not need to engage in all possible battles. While there are important battles to fight that are necessary to defend our rights and achieve important objectives, we must avoid unnecessary battles. If we do not have clear strategies for selecting confrontations, our life becomes a series of battles.

These confrontations consume our energy, disrupt our lives, and add to the number of our enemies.

Even when we do have clear objectives, priorities, and plans, we can still be entangled in battles that go against those objectives and plans. This can happen for reasons such as personal or professional biases, or just for the sake of confrontation. An individual could create a major confrontation simply by saying the wrong thing, sending the wrong letter, or perhaps including an unnecessary sentence in a good letter. Such a simple action could create confrontations that divert attention away from the objective at hand.

Nations can also be entangled in poorly thought out confrontations that can turn into major wars. These wars can waste resources and harm many people. Artificial objectives and slogans are usually cited afterwards to justify such wars and their resulting killing and maiming of innocent people.

Our time is valuable and our resources are precious. It is high time for us to redirect our efforts and resources away from unnecessary confrontations that spoil our lives and distract us from worthy and noble objectives.

PART TWO: ELEMENTS OF THE BALANCED WAY

Opting for Constructive Dialogue

While our feelings towards others create a logical basis for the continuity of our relationship with them, our assumptions about the feelings others have towards us must be dealt with carefully, for they could be false. We cannot see into people's hearts and minds to be sure of their real feelings towards us.

The best and simplest way to avoid misunderstandings and to be sure of our assumptions regarding people's feelings towards us is to engage in constructive dialogue. However, major obstacles can get in the way of constructive dialogue. These obstacles include pride, stubbornness, and prejudice.

I had a long relationship with a dear friend, during which we had many happy times. Our relationship, however, was repeatedly interrupted by periods of intense quarrels and painful misunderstandings that were usually triggered by my doubts as to how much my friend admired me or respected our friendship. Luckily, those instances did not destroy our relationship; but many times, it teetered on the verge of total collapse.

In a recent conversation with my friend about our disputes long ago, I was astonished to hear him say that his major source of frustration at the time of our disputes resulted from his doubts about my admiration for him or for our friendship. Years after costly and hurtful disputes, we discovered, in a matter of minutes, that there was no real reason for our past quarrels and unhappiness. That discovery was a result of constructive and mature dialogue where each of us overcame pride and stubbornness. Having such an open conversation a long time ago to clear up a basic issue could have saved us tremendous agony and kept our friendship from such risk.

> *"Every story has three sides to it —*
> *yours, mine and the facts."*
>
> —Foster Meharny Russell

This incident showed me how wrong our assumptions about others can be and how our feelings of pride, stubbornness, and prejudice can threaten important relationships. Such incorrect or unverified assumptions have, in many cases, led to the collapse of friendships, families, and organizations.

While pride and prejudice can get in the way of openness and positive dialogue between friends and families, other obstacles can also stand in the way of positive dialogue between societies and nations. Those obstacles could include differences in culture, experiences, and history. Those differences, however, should not impede dialogue between societies and nations, but rather be a source of richer understanding.

> *"O you people, we have created you of man and woman and made you into nations and tribes so that you might come to know one another. The most noble among you before God are the ones who are most righteous."*

—Qur'an, 49:13

Expecting Goodness from Others

Giving others the benefit of the doubt or expecting goodness from them is not merely the demonstration of a positive attitude, but rather an important principle on both personal and organizational levels. As was true for expecting good things from God, expecting goodness from others carries with it numerous benefits.

Before addressing the benefits of expecting goodness from others, a misconception about this principle must be cleared. Expecting goodness from others is commonly associated with naiveté and with not protecting our interests. Thus, many of us opt for (or are advised of) not trusting others until they prove they are trustworthy. A fine but important difference exists between the two. Naiveté and forsaking one's interest is a characteristic associated with weakness and an inability to protect one's interests. Expecting goodness from others, on the other hand, is a mature and conscious choice based upon strength and the ability to protect one's interests. Strong, mature, and confident individuals can afford to expect goodness from others and give them the benefit of the doubt. Strong people are aware of their rights so that others do not easily take advantage of them. Even when others attempt to do so, mature and confident individuals are capable of protecting their interests.

Expecting goodness from others creates wonderful advantages on individual, social, and professional levels that make it worth the effort. On a personal level, expecting goodness and giving the benefit of the doubt to family members and friends creates an environment of peace and trust. This environment strengthens the cohesion of these relations, leads to more transparency and constructive dialogue, supports good relations, and spreads a sense of serenity. Such a state cannot take place when doubt, mistrust, and lack of transparency or dialogue are present.

PART TWO: ELEMENTS OF THE BALANCED WAY

"Trust men and they will be true to you; treat them greatly and they will show themselves great."

—*Ralph Waldo Emerson*

On a professional level, expecting goodness from colleagues and business associates and giving them the benefit of the doubt lead to higher levels of communication, cooperation, and productivity. Mistrust, protectionism, and lack of transparency within the business environment are among the characteristics of "unhealthy companies," something that I will address later.[29]

Reaping the benefits of expecting goodness from others on various levels of our lives has to be coupled, as indicated above, with a conscious effort not to give others the opportunity, or encourage them, to take advantage of us.

Case Study:
In light of a long and fruitful relationship between a grocery store owner and a meat supplier, and in an effort to improve his business, the meat supplier proposed a five-year exclusivity agreement with the grocery store owner. The deal looked

---

[29] "He who mistrusts most should be trusted least," Theognis, 540-480 B.C. Quoted in John M. Shanahan, *The Most Brilliant Thoughts of All Times* (New York: HarperCollins Publishers, Inc, 2005), 230.

good to the grocery store owner, for it gave him the high quality of meat he was used to with even more advantageous prices and service. Knowing the reliability and trustworthiness of the meat supplier, and following the principal of "expecting goodness from others," the owner of the grocery store signed the agreement.

Two years later, the owner of the grocery store discovered that the meat supply company had been acquired by one of his competitors. The new owner of the meat company changed the quality of the product, raised prices, and altered delivery services so that the arrangement was no longer suitable for the grocery store. Being bound by the exclusivity agreement for three more years became a major problem for the grocery store owner, which then led to litigation and a waste of money and energy.

From the above case study, two questions arise:

1. Was the grocery store owner wrong in adopting the policy of giving the benefit of the doubt and expecting goodness from others?

2. If expecting goodness from others is a good policy to follow, why did the grocery store owner get into such a problematic situation?

PART TWO: ELEMENTS OF THE BALANCED WAY

Looking again at the situation, the grocery store owner's lack of judgment was not in expecting goodness and giving the benefit of the doubt to the meat supplier, but rather in not doing proper due diligence before signing the agreement. The grocery store owner hastily signed the agreement. He did not write in any clauses protecting him in case of a change in ownership of the meat company. Nor did he include detailed specifications about the quality of the products and delivery services he expected. Because he was not protected, it was possible for the new owner to change the quality of the products and the delivery system radically.

If the grocery store owner had done his homework, he would have requested the inclusion of such clauses. Having good intentions, the meat supplier would not have rejected them. If he had rejected them, the grocery store owner would have received a clear sign that it was a bad deal, and he would have been spared the agony of signing a bad agreement. Even if he had not signed this agreement, the grocery store owner could still have enjoyed the mutually beneficial relationship between the two parties that was already ongoing based upon good expectations and trust.

This case study demonstrates the difference between expecting goodness from others on the one side and naiveté, forsaking our interest, and not doing our homework on the other. Being careless and not protecting our interest gets in the way of benefiting from the principle of expecting goodness from others. It also promotes misconceptions about expecting goodness from others that in turn promotes distrust and hinders communication and potential cooperation.

The positive attitudes of expecting goodness from others, giving them the benefit of the doubt, and promoting kindness in general can actually change the attitude of people we deal with from hostile to friendly, from cutthroat to positive competitors, and from enemies to friends. We should not dismiss people at the first sign of hostility or bad attitude. The benefits of expecting goodness from others, giving them the benefit of the doubt, and hence, promoting goodness and kindness are truly incalculable.

> *"Respond in a better way; then will the one between whom and thee was enmity become as though he was a close friend."*
>
> —Qur'an, 41:34

Escaping the Success Trap

Being proud of our successes and achievements is a natural human phenomenon. For some people, this feeling of pride is coupled with a sense of urgency to maintain the same or higher levels of success and a sense of humility about their level of achievements compared to others who have achieved more. Success also can lead to a feeling of superiority over others who have not achieved similar levels of success. This feeling of superiority towards others is a clear sign of arrogance and an inability to see the value of our achievements within the context of our universe.

> *"When we fail, our pride supports us;
> when we succeed, it betrays us."*
>
> *—Charles Caleb Colton*

In addition to offending others and blinding us to ways to improve, being too proud and arrogant has a negative impact on our future. Shakespeare has clearly depicted such a case in Julius Caesar's "North Star" speech,[30] and in Caesar's eventual destiny. In this speech, Caesar compares himself to the North Star that is a steadfast guide for all humankind. This statement of excessive pride comes before Caesar's murder by his closest friends and associates. A similar story is told of the *Titanic*, when the designers boasted that even God himself

---

30 William Shakespeare (*Julius Caesar*, III, I, 60–62).

could not sink it. I know of two successful multimillionaires who were so confident of their continued success and wealth that they challenged poverty to catch up with them. Each of them soon after felt the pinch of hard time. One of those individuals was a victim of the 2008 worldwide economic crisis.

Humility on the other hand brings good fortune,[31] appreciation, and support from others. It is always useful to remember, from time to time, that we live in a galaxy in which there are more than a billion other solar systems like ours. There are also one hundred billion galaxies if not more, similar to ours in the universe. Remembering these facts should give us a vivid sense of how insignificant our planet is when compared to the universe. When we remember the relatively minute size of our planet, we realize that we cannot achieve anything of significance, relative to the scale of the universe, even if we have the whole planet earth to ourselves, let alone if we share it with six billion others.

> *"Modesty is a shining light; it prepares the mind to receive knowledge, and the heart for truth."*
>
> —*Madam Guizot*

---

[31] "He who is humble before God will be brought up to a higher rank," (a *Tradition of Prophet Mohammed*).

PART TWO: ELEMENTS OF THE BALANCED WAY

Road Signs on the Path

My Priorities

- Do I have a list of my priorities in life? Do I think deeply about them?

- Do I sometimes feel that I am inattentive to my work due to social or personal reasons?

- Do I sometimes feel that my work or any other activity is taking too much time away from my family and loved ones?

- Are some of my current projects or interests not conducive to achieving balance in my personal, social, professional, and spiritual realms?

Choosing My Battles

- Do I find myself a part of repeated confrontations with people I deal with or with people close to me that affect my relationships with them negatively?

- Do I receive any benefits from my repeated confrontations with others?

- Can I think of the reasons that usually lead to such confrontations?

- Can I learn ways to limit my confrontations with others?

Positive Dialogue

- Do repeated misunderstandings arise between people I care about and me?

- Do I sometimes feel that pride prevents me from talking openly about issues? How can I overcome that feeling of pride and achieve higher levels of communication?

- Can I specify the actions I take or comments I normally make that create such misunderstandings, and can I avoid them?

- Can my loved ones and I go into an open dialogue as one team with the aim of eliminating any source of miscommunication in a way that brings higher levels of happiness and stability to our relationship?

- Do I feel bad when I remember people I have wronged? Can I contact them to apologize and resolve previous misunderstandings?

Expecting Goodness from Others

- Do I have a tendency to distrust others?

- If distrusting others has resulted from previous bad experiences, was it because I made it easy for them to take advantage of me?

- How can I enhance my ability to trust others, while at the same time not making it easy for them to take advantage of me?

- Is there a predominant feeling of distrust among the employees of the company I work for? If so, am I in a position to improve the level of trust among the employees, to the extent that more communication and a better work environment are prevalent within the company?

Escaping the Success Trap

- Do I occasionally feel that I need to remind others about my distinctions?

- Is my need for recognition resulting from feeling that people do not appreciate my achievements, or is it just because I want to remind them that I am the best?

- Can I stop eliciting praise or indicating my distinction over others and see how they respond to that?

- Do I feel that I am better than others who have a lower professional status than I do?

- Can I imagine life if others, regardless of their professional level, did not play their roles?

- Can I always remember my position in this vast universe?

PART TWO: ELEMENTS OF THE BALANCED WAY

5. Maintaining High Ethical Standards on Personal and Professional Levels

"Happiness is when what you think, what you say, and what you do are in harmony."

—*Mahatma Gandhi*

Moral Values from Individual to Organizational Levels

Years ago, I read in a Western book on Middle Eastern cities that the origin of the word "risk" in the English language goes back to an Arabic word "rizq." This word means "God's bounty." Merchants in the Middle East used this word to represent income from trade, indicating that they conducted commercial activities as a means of earning God's bounty. The word "rizq" is said to have been translated thereafter

THE BALANCED WAY

into "risk" in English, indicating that commercial activities are based upon taking risks for obtaining more profits.

Notwithstanding the relationship between the two words, Muslim merchants believe that "rizq" (income) is ultimately allocated by God, and that honestly-earned profits lead to blessed income. Income is blessed in the sense that it is protected from waste and leads to prosperity and good fortune. Seeking blessed income has made it incumbent on merchants, who are eager to earn it, to adopt honesty and fair dealing in their commercial transactions.

While applying notions such as "blessing" as a basis for higher moral behavior can seem somewhat remote to the nature of organizations, international corporations have tried during the last few decades to adopt higher levels of professional and moral ethics as part of their corporate culture.[32] The aim of these efforts is to enhance performance, accountability, corporate governance, and social responsibility, which will lead to sustainable benefits and prosperity for the company and society as a whole. In their book *Diagnosing and Changing the Culture of Companies*, Kim Cameron and

---

[32] The Savola Group, the company where I am a board member, has adopted four core principles as part of its "Balanced Way" approach. These core principles are: honesty, which drives responsibility towards shareholders; conscientiousness, which drives responsibility towards clients, suppliers, and the community as a whole; caring justice, which drives responsibility towards employees; and personal control, which drives self-improvement and self-discipline.

PART TWO: ELEMENTS OF THE BALANCED WAY

Robert Quinn indicate that in the 1960s, modern management focused on the product; in the 1970s, the focus was on the market; in the 1980s it was on the customer; and in the 1990s, the focus was on the company itself. The focus of organizations since the 1990s, according to the two authors, is on the culture of organizations.

In their best-selling book *Built to Last: Successful Habits of Visionary Companies*, and in light of a detailed study of eighteen leading companies, James Collins and Jerry Porras show how a "core value" structure is a common ingredient in successful companies.

Applying high moral values at the organizational level brings numerous benefits to the company. These can include improved corporate reputation, increased confidence in the company's products, increased employee performance, enhanced employee morale and loyalty to the company, and other benefits.

Following strict moral conduct and good corporate governance as integral parts of companies' culture are becoming more crucial with time. This is especially important in light of major corporate scandals such as those of Enron and WorldCom, not to mention the 2008 sub-prime mortgage crisis, which has led to the collapse of major institutions, huge losses to homeowners and shareholders, and a threat to the stability of world economy.

The Culture of Companies and Employees' Ethics

Our professional environment can sometimes challenge our pursuit of higher professional standards. The culture of companies has its way of somehow, directly or indirectly, influencing the behavior and ethics of individuals within these companies. While the environment within an organization can transform an inefficient employee into an efficient one, an organization can also have a negative impact on its employees' ethical values. In this respect, "healthy" organizations bring out the best in their employees. These companies have, among other things, moral codes to regulate relations with shareholders, employees, other organizations, and the community at large. These "healthy" organizations also use their employees' best abilities. They stimulate their competitive capacity and team spirit towards the achievement of higher levels of efficiency and moral behavior.

"Unhealthy" organizations, on the other hand, are characterized, among other things, by their disregard for professional ethics, and/or assigning positions and giving incentives to individuals who do not deserve them. This makes hypocrisy the only way of showing performance, devious behavior the only means of competition among the employees, and efficiency a low priority.

PART TWO: ELEMENTS OF THE BALANCED WAY

Top executives of companies have a moral responsibility to create an organizational culture that improves the ability, behavior, and moral conduct of their employees, and does *not* push employees towards adopting negative behavior that could change the good nature with which God created them.[33]

The following is an example of values and attitudes outlining the culture of a company seeking a high standard of corporate ethics.

Our Corporate Culture

- We work diligently on securing higher profits for our shareholders through conducting activities with high efficiency and through the pursuit of fruitful relations with our partners and companies with which we deal.

- We are committed to truthfulness, honesty, and transparency in dealing with our colleagues, our customers, our partners, and society; even if it is at the cost of efforts and profits.

---

[33] "We have indeed created man in the best form. Then we reduced him to the lowest of low. Except for those who believe and do righteous deeds: they shall receive endless reward," (*Qur'an* 95:4–6).

- We seek justice and fairness in dealing with our colleagues, our employees, our shareholders, our customers, and our business partners.

- We expect good intentions from others while working hard to protect our own interests.

- We do not make any decisions that could negatively affect the communities and the natural environment in which we operate.

Our Ethical Tool Kit

During the 1990s, I taught professional practice and ethics to architectural students. At the end of every course, I gave my students what I called "The Ethical Tool Kit." This was a technique for making an instant judgment about certain decisions we might make and about how ethical they might be. The following case study explores the intent and application of this "kit."

While evaluating proposals from various suppliers, Ali noticed how close the proposals were in terms of prices and quality. During this period of evaluation, Ali met a friend who informed him indirectly that one of the suppliers was willing to pay for a personal trip for him and his family if he overlooked one of the conditions that this supplier did not satisfy.

Ali faced a dilemma in making a decision to award the contract to the supplier related to his friend. Overlooking the condition of this supplier would not affect his company negatively, and no one would even notice it. In trying to arrive at a decision, Ali referred to the following principle:

> *"Sin [unethical] is that which wavers in your heart and you do not want people to find out about it."*[34]

Thinking about how he felt about awarding the contract to this company, he realized that he felt uncomfortable; however, knowing that awarding the contract to this company would not affect his company negatively, made him feel more comfortable about awarding the contract to that specific supplier.

In order to arrive at the right decision, Ali followed the second step of the principle, which is related to whether he would feel good about letting his colleagues, his family, or others know about the basis for awarding the contract to

---

[34] Prophet Mohammed. Narrated by Muslim, *Sahih Muslim* (Riyadh: Darussalam, 2007, 423).

THE BALANCED WAY

this supplier. Thinking about this made it very clear to him that awarding the contract to this supplier would not be ethical, since he would not be comfortable with letting others know about the basis for awarding this contract to this company.

PART TWO: ELEMENTS OF THE BALANCED WAY

Road Signs on the Path

- Do I sometimes face conflicts between my attitudes or professional conducts and my personal moral values?

- Do I feel that I must sometimes ignore unethical actions my boss or colleagues take, just for the sake of keeping things moving at work?

- Do I inform my colleagues that I do not accept unethical actions and that following a higher moral conduct should not hurt our company if our objectives are right?

- If my position in the company does not allow me to change its professional environment for the better, are there other opportunities for me to work in a different company?

- Do I have an "Ethical Tool Kit" that can guide me in making choices and decisions on matters not ethically clear to me?

PART TWO: ELEMENTS OF THE BALANCED WAY

6. Taking the Initiative

> *"The beginning is the most important part of the work."*
>
> *—Plato*

WE always have the choice of being in the driver's seat and positively influencing our lives or being passive and dependant on what others do. By not taking the initiative in positively influencing our life, we lose many opportunities for self-improvement. It also gives others the opportunity to influence our life in a way suitable and convenient to them.

A positive relationship exists between achieving our objectives on the one hand, and our ability to take the initiative on the other. On an organizational level, a company that does not continuously improve its ability to compete will eventually lose its edge and cease to exist. On the other hand, having a clear strategy for development, keeping an eye on competitors and socio-economic changes, and taking appropriate initiatives, puts companies in a solid position to compete and achieve higher levels of success.

On an individual level, the ability to achieve higher levels of excellence and contentment requires following a strategy that maintains a balance among different aspects of life as well as having clear objectives, in light of which, positive initiatives can be taken. Establishing a clear strategy requires answering some basic questions (whether consciously or unconsciously). These questions could include the following:

- What are the accomplishments in my personal, professional, social, and spiritual realms that should be satisfactory to me if I happened to die tomorrow?[35]

- Do I feel content about my life and about what God has given me?

---

[35] "Our repugnance to death increases in proportion to our consciousness of having lived in vain," William Hazlitt, 1778 – 1830. Quoted in John M. Shanahan, *The Most Brilliant Thoughts of all times* (New York: HarperCollins Publishers, Inc, 2005), 287.

PART TWO: ELEMENTS OF THE BALANCED WAY

- How can I achieve higher levels on both grounds?

Answering such questions will provide us with a global view of our lives and ways to reach higher levels of excellence and contentment. In light of those answers, we can specify different sets of questions to answer in areas that require further improvements.

"The unexamined life is not worth living."

—Socrates

Establishing a clear vision of what we are planning to achieve will provide us with positive energy. We can use this energy to reflect on the future and work on shaping it in the way we want, instead of dwelling on negative thoughts and complaining about not being "lucky."

Specifying objectives, taking initiatives, and making positive changes at various levels of our lives must also be accompanied by persistence whenever our plans face challenges.

THE BALANCED WAY

Road Signs on the Path

- Do I, every now and then, take time to reflect on my life, try to answer some nagging questions about how it is going, and think about how to improve it?

- Can I, from this moment, specify things to do, on my own or with others, which could give me higher levels of excellence and contentment?

PART THREE: TOWARDS A BALANCED WAY

1. The Balanced Way: An Ongoing Development Process

2. My Path to Excellence and Contentment

PART THREE: TOWARDS A BALANCED WAY

1. The Balanced Way: An Ongoing Development Process

IN exploring the path to excellence and contentment, we began by revisiting our definition of success and our notions of happiness and contentment. Based upon this exploration, we established that happiness is not achieved by getting what we want, whether it is success or having things go our way, but rather by the satisfaction of getting those things. Satisfaction with success or having things go our way has, however, the tendency of fading away and taking with it the happiness we thought we had.

Relying on success or having things go our way as our only way to achieving happiness could lead to unhappiness when we do not achieve those conditions that make us "happy" as frequently as we need. A more sustainable state of happiness can be achieved by being content with ourselves, our lives, and with what God has given us.

THE BALANCED WAY

Achieving a sustainable state of excellence and contentment requires maintaining balance between two seemingly contradictory conditions. These conditions are; accepting our life and what we have, and not being fully satisfied with our previous achievements. Without this state of balance, we will experience one of two extremes. The first is having success (or things going our way) as our only source of "happiness" and peace of mind that can lead to frustration and despair whenever our plans do not succeed. The other extreme is to rely on the success we have achieved, lose the desire to push ourselves, and, hence, stagnate and fall into idleness, which might lead to misery and lack of happiness.

Maintaining this state of balance requires taking a series of steps. These steps include establishing a balanced perception of reality, a positive outlook on the future, and liberating ourselves from the past with all its associated pain, frustration, and jealousy. We need this balanced state of mind to improve our sense of reality, limit our fears of the future, and enhance our acceptance of ourselves and our past—with its successes and failures, and with what God has given us. Without such attitudes towards our reality, our past, our future, and ourselves, contentment cannot be achieved.

Developing this state of mind must be coupled with taking positive actions regarding various aspects of our life.

PART THREE: TOWARDS A BALANCED WAY

This process includes dealing positively with problems, adopting balanced attitudes, maintaining high ethical standards on personal and professional levels, and taking positive initiatives to change our life for the better.

The balanced way is hence a process rather than a specific objective. It aims at achieving various levels of balance on mental, personal, social, professional, moral, and spiritual levels.

PART THREE: TOWARDS A BALANCED WAY

2. My Path to Excellence and Contentment

IN enhancing and stimulating this developmental process towards a higher level of balance, a series of questions were posed as "Road Signs on the Path." Answering the questions posed in the Road Signs or similar questions on a regular basis and exploring alternatives to what we can do about them, in light of our own experience and the ideas explored in the previous chapters, is very important in this developmental process.

To make this exercise more specific and usable, I provided a set of matrixes in Appendix I. These matrixes can depict your current position and lead to where you want to be on the path to excellence and contentment. These positions and aspirations can be recorded and revisited towards further future progress. In these matrixes, your response to each of the questions can be indicated by Yes or No. The intensity of the response, whether Yes or a No, is made by circling a number

THE BALANCED WAY

from one to five (one representing a strong Yes, and five representing a strong No). A column titled "Status," where you can summarize your current position in reference to any specific Road Sign, follows this response. After recording your position in relation to the Road Sign, in the following column "The Next Point on the Path," you can specify what you need to do in light of your own experience and the ideas explored in the previous chapters, in order to reach a higher level on the path to excellence and contentment.

EXAMPLE

Road Signs	Yes				No	Status	The Next Point on the Path
If my definition of success is based only upon society's appreciation of me and of my achievements, are there other achievements that I can accomplish for my own personal satisfaction?	①	2	3	4	5	*I have always had an interest in helping the homeless, which I kept putting off for various reasons. Doing that should give me high personal satisfaction and make me feel better about my life.*	*Contact organizations that help the homeless. Become an active member of (or work for) such an organization before the end of this year.*

PART THREE: TOWARDS A BALANCED WAY

Road Signs	Yes		No			Status	The Next Point on the Path
Does dissatisfaction with my previous achievements or my inability to achieve the success I want or deserve make me vulnerable and discontented with my life?	1	②	3	4	5	It's mostly so	Establish a balance between what I want and what I have. Enhance my acceptance of myself, my past, and what God gave me. Expect good things from the future while increasing my efforts to achieve the success I want and deserve.
Do I hear, from time to time, somebody telling me, "Things are not as bad as you think"?	①	2	3	4	5	I hear that from my friends and family members.	Make a list of all the good things I have, compared to others in the world. Be more grateful for what I have and optimistic about what I will have that will give me more contentment and launch the Power of Expectation in my favor.

THE BALANCED WAY

While all the Road Signs related to each of the elements of the balanced way are included in Appendix I, you can select your own matrixes to pursue. You can also make a photocopy of matrixes with the selected topics, so that you can do the exercise every now and then to gauge progress in achieving a particular level. If you prefer to keep the exercise as part of the book, you can use a pencil in recording "Status" and the "Next Point on the Path." Then you can revisit, revise, and modify the matrixes as regularly as you like.

It is understandable that each reader will have her or his own path or Road Signs, some of which might not have been included in the matrixes. For this purpose, I have provided a blank matrix in Appendix II that can be copied and used from time to time to record the status of your own personal Road Signs and the next level you choose to specify.

The optimal point you can reach following this process occurs when the questions of your personally selected Road Signs occur to you regularly, and when you find that the latest answers are close to the state you want to reach on the path to excellence and contentment. At such a point, there will be no need to use the matrixes, as you will have your own internal matrix with your own path and Road Signs.

I hope you enjoy and benefit from this process.

Appendix I

My Current and Future Positions on the Path

My Definition of Success

Road Signs	Yes	No	Status	The Next Point on the Path
Is my definition of success based upon achieving higher levels of acceptance in my society?	1 2 3	4 5		

THE BALANCED WAY

Road Signs	Yes			No		Status	The Next Point on the Path
If my definition of success is only based upon society's acceptance and appreciation of my achievements, are there other personal, social, academic, professional, or spiritual achievements, which I can accomplish that could also give me personal satisfaction?	1	2	3	4	5		

APPENDIX I: MY CURRENT AND FUTURE POSITIONS

Road Signs	Yes			No		Status	The Next Point on the Path
Does society's definition of success have no place in my definition of success? Is this because I do not care, I know better, or because I enjoy defying society's values and norms?	1	2	3	4	5		

THE BALANCED WAY

Road Signs	Yes		No		Status	The Next Point on the Path
Can I strike a balance between my personal notion of success and society's broadly accepted definition of success in a way that can benefit me and my society?	1	2	3	4 5		

APPENDIX I: MY CURRENT AND FUTURE POSITIONS

Balancing My Formula of Excellence and Contentment

Road Signs	Yes			No		Status	The Next Point on the Path
Does dissatisfaction with my previous achievements and my strong desire to achieve higher levels of success make me vulnerable and discontented?	1	2	3	4	5		

THE BALANCED WAY

Road Signs	Yes			No		Status	The Next Point on the Path
Is success as I define it, or having things go my way, my only source of happiness and satisfaction?	1	2	3	4	5		

APPENDIX I: MY CURRENT AND FUTURE POSITIONS

Road Signs	Yes				No	Status	The Next Point on the Path
	1	2	3	4	5		
Do I feel miserable, frustrated, or hopeless when my efforts to achieve success face challenges?							

THE BALANCED WAY

Road Signs	Yes	No	Status	The Next Point on the Path
Do I hear, from time to time, somebody telling me "be grateful for what you have"?	1 2 3	4 5		

APPENDIX I: MY CURRENT AND FUTURE POSITIONS

Road Signs	Yes			No		Status	The Next Point on the Path
Can I enhance my feelings of contentment in a way that gives me a higher level of internal stability and protects me from despair when my efforts to achieve success face challenges?	1	2	3	4	5		

THE BALANCED WAY

Improving My Perception of Reality

Road Signs	Yes	No	Status	The Next Point on the Path
Do I feel that I have a negative perception of reality?	1 2 3	4 5		

APPENDIX I: MY CURRENT AND FUTURE POSITIONS

Road Signs	Yes			No		Status	The Next Point on the Path
Do people tell me, from time to time, that the situation is not as bad as I think it is?	1	2	3	4	5		

THE BALANCED WAY

Road Signs	Yes			No		Status	The Next Point on the Path
Do I notice that people avoid me when I complain or when I make negative comments about myself or others?	1	2	3	4	5		

APPENDIX I: MY CURRENT AND FUTURE POSITIONS

Road Signs	Yes			No		Status	The Next Point on the Path
Knowing that my state of mind shapes my reality; can I improve the way I look at reality?	1	2	3	4	5		

THE BALANCED WAY

Enhancing My Outlook to the Future

Road Signs	Yes	No	Status	The Next Point on the Path
Do I find myself in a continuous state of fear of the future?	1 2	3 4 5		

APPENDIX I: MY CURRENT AND FUTURE POSITIONS

Road Signs	Yes	No	Status	The Next Point on the Path
Does trusting God with my life and the lives of the people I love give me a higher level of contentment and peace of mind?	1 2 3	4 5		

THE BALANCED WAY

Road Signs	Yes			No		Status	The Next Point on the Path
Can I improve my expectations of God's mercy and kindness?	1	2	3	4	5		

APPENDIX I: MY CURRENT AND FUTURE POSITIONS

Liberating myself from the Shackles of the Past

Road Signs	Yes			No		Status	The Next Point on the Path
Do I experience feelings of sadness or frustration when I remember past failures and bad events?	1	2	3	4	5		

THE BALANCED WAY

Road Signs	Yes			No			Status	The Next Point on the Path
Do I regularly have a nagging feeling that bad things should not have happened or feel responsible for not changing them into something better?	1	2	3	4	5			

APPENDIX I: MY CURRENT AND FUTURE POSITIONS

Road Signs	Yes			No		Status	The Next Point on the Path
Can I reinforce my acceptance of destiny to the extent that gives me a higher level of contentment and liberates me from my feelings of sorrow, pain, anger, or responsibility for not changing what has happened in the past?	1	2	3	4	5		

THE BALANCED WAY

Road Signs	Yes	No	Status	The Next Point on the Path
Do I feel contented and free when I perform my deep breathing exercise or a similar technique?	1 2 3	4 5		

APPENDIX I: MY CURRENT AND FUTURE POSITIONS

Road Signs	Yes			No		Status	The Next Point on the Path
If the breathing exercise (or any similar technique) does not give me a sufficient level of contentment, is that because I do not want to free myself from the past pains and agonies?	1	2	3	4	5		

THE BALANCED WAY

Road Signs	Yes			No			Status	The Next Point on the Path
Can I work harder to change my attitude towards the past?	1	2	3	4	5			

APPENDIX I: MY CURRENT AND FUTURE POSITIONS

Road Signs	Yes			No		Status	The Next Point on the Path
Can I benefit from my experiences in avoiding new failures?	1	2	3	4	5		

THE BALANCED WAY

Road Signs	Yes	No	Status	The Next Point on the Path
Do I occasionally feel frustrated and jealous of others who have achieved certain successes or acquired things I did not get?	1 2 3	4 5		

APPENDIX I: MY CURRENT AND FUTURE POSITIONS

Road Signs	Yes	No	Status	The Next Point on the Path
Do I feel that what others have received, I should have received too?	1 2 3	4 5		

THE BALANCED WAY

Road Signs	Yes	No	Status	The Next Point on the Path
Knowing that what others have received, whether it was good or bad, was meant to happen regardless of what they or others could have done, can I be happy about the good things that have happened to them and remember that thinking positively about what they got will bring good things to me?	1 2 3	4 5		

APPENDIX I: MY CURRENT AND FUTURE POSITIONS

Dealing with My Problems

Road Signs	Yes			No		Status	The Next Point on the Path
Do I occasionally find myself unable to deal with my problems?	1	2	3	4	5		

THE BALANCED WAY

Road Signs	Yes	No	Status	The Next Point on the Path
Do I sometimes talk about my problems and my bad luck in an attempt to win others' sympathy or to justify my failures?	1 2 3	4 5		

APPENDIX I: MY CURRENT AND FUTURE POSITIONS

Road Signs	Yes				No	Status	The Next Point on the Path
Do I feel frustrated and depressed when I face problems to the extent that I am unable to deal with them?	1	2	3	4	5		

THE BALANCED WAY

Road Signs	Yes	No	Status	The Next Point on the Path
Can I follow the proactive approach of dealing with problems or a similar approach towards solving them?	1 2 3	4 5		

APPENDIX I: MY CURRENT AND FUTURE POSITIONS

Road Signs	Yes			No		Status	The Next Point on the Path
If I cannot resolve some of my problems, can I at least achieve a state of coexistence with them?	1	2	3	4	5		

Balancing My Priorities

Road Signs	Yes			No	Status	The Next Point on the Path
Do I have a list of my priorities in life? Do I think deeply about them?	1	2	3	4	5		

APPENDIX I: MY CURRENT AND FUTURE POSITIONS

Road Signs	Yes			No		Status	The Next Point on the Path
Do I sometimes feel that I am inattentive to my work due to social or personal reasons?	1	2	3	4	5		

THE BALANCED WAY

Road Signs	Yes	No	Status	The Next Point on the Path
Do I sometimes feel that my work or any other activity is taking too much time away from my family and loved ones?	1 2 3	4 5		

APPENDIX I: MY CURRENT AND FUTURE POSITIONS

Road Signs	Yes	No	Status	The Next Point on the Path
Are some of my current projects or interest not conducive to achieving balance in my personal, social, professional, and spiritual realms?	1 2 3	4 5		

THE BALANCED WAY

Choosing My Battles

Road Signs	Yes	No	Status	The Next Point on the Path
Do I find myself a part of repeated confrontations with people I deal with or with people close to me that affect my relationships with them negatively?	1 2	3 4 5		

APPENDIX I: MY CURRENT AND FUTURE POSITIONS

Road Signs	Yes	No	Status	The Next Point on the Path
Do I receive any benefits from my repeated confrontations with others?	1 2 3	4 5		

THE BALANCED WAY

Road Signs	Yes			No		Status	The Next Point on the Path
Can I think of the reasons that usually lead to such confrontations?	1	2	3	4	5		

APPENDIX I: MY CURRENT AND FUTURE POSITIONS

Road Signs	Yes			No		Status	The Next Point on the Path
Can I learn ways to limit my confrontations with others?	1	2	3	4	5		

THE BALANCED WAY

Opting for Positive Dialogue

Road Signs	Yes	No	Status	The Next Point on the Path
Do repeated misunderstandings arise between people I care about and me?	1 2 3	4 5		

APPENDIX I: MY CURRENT AND FUTURE POSITIONS

Road Signs	Yes			No		Status	The Next Point on the Path
	1	2	3	4	5		
Do I sometimes feel that pride prevents me from talking openly about issues? How can I overcome that feeling of pride and achieve higher levels of communication?							

THE BALANCED WAY

Road Signs	Yes	No	Status	The Next Point on the Path
Can I specify the actions I take or comments I normally make that create such misunderstandings, and can I avoid them?	1 2 3	4 5		

APPENDIX I: MY CURRENT AND FUTURE POSITIONS

Road Signs	Yes			No		Status	The Next Point on the Path
Can my loved ones and I go into an open dialogue as one team with the aim of eliminating any source of miscommunication in a way that brings higher levels of happiness and stability to our relationship?	1	2	3	4	5		

THE BALANCED WAY

Road Signs	Yes			No		Status	The Next Point on the Path
Do I feel bad when I remember people I have wronged? Can I contact them to apologize and resolve previous misunderstandings?	1	2	3	4	5		

APPENDIX I: MY CURRENT AND FUTURE POSITIONS

Expecting Goodness from Others

Road Signs	Yes	No	Status	The Next Point on the Path
Do I have a tendency to distrust others?	1 2 3	4 5		

THE BALANCED WAY

Road Signs	Yes			No		Status	The Next Point on the Path
If distrusting others has resulted from previous bad experiences, was it because I made it easy for them to take advantage of me?	1	2	3	4	5		

APPENDIX I: MY CURRENT AND FUTURE POSITIONS

Road Signs	Yes				No	Status	The Next Point on the Path
Can I enhance my ability to trust others, while at the same time not making it easy for them to take advantage of me?	1	2	3	4	5		

THE BALANCED WAY

Road Signs	Yes	No	Status	The Next Point on the Path
Is there a predominant feeling of distrust among the employees of the company I work for? If so, am I in a position to improve the level of trust among the employees, to the extent that more communication and a better work environment are prevalent within the company?	1 2 3	4 5		

APPENDIX I: MY CURRENT AND FUTURE POSITIONS

Escaping the Success Trap

Road Signs	Yes	No	Status	The Next Point on the Path
Do I occasionally feel that I need to remind others about my distinctions?	1 2 3	4 5		

THE BALANCED WAY

Road Signs	Yes	No	Status	The Next Point on the Path
Is my need for recognition resulting from feeling that people do not appreciate my achievements?	1 2	3 4 5		

APPENDIX I: MY CURRENT AND FUTURE POSITIONS

Road Signs	Yes				No	Status	The Next Point on the Path
Do I feel furious when people do not give me due praise, and instead praise others who are not worthy of it?	1	2	3	4	5		

THE BALANCED WAY

Road Signs	Yes		No			Status	The Next Point on the Path
Has it occurred to me that my persistence in eliciting people's appreciation is a major reason behind their lack of appreciation of me compared to others?	1	2	3	4	5		

APPENDIX I: MY CURRENT AND FUTURE POSITIONS

Road Signs	Yes				No	Status	The Next Point on the Path
Do I sometimes feel that others avoid me when I elicit their appreciation or when I imply that I am better than they are?	1	2	3	4	5		

THE BALANCED WAY

Road Signs	Yes	No	Status	The Next Point on the Path
Can I stop eliciting praise or indicating my distinction over others and see how they respond to that?	1 2 3	4 5		

APPENDIX I: MY CURRENT AND FUTURE POSITIONS

Road Signs	Yes				No	Status	The Next Point on the Path
Do I feel that I am better than others who have a lower professional status than I do?	1	2	3	4	5		

THE BALANCED WAY

Road Signs	Yes	No	Status	The Next Point on the Path
Can I imagine life if others, regardless of their professional level, did not play their roles?	1 2 3	3 4 5		

APPENDIX I: MY CURRENT AND FUTURE POSITIONS

Road Signs	Yes			No		Status	The Next Point on the Path
	1	2	3	4	5		
Can I always remember my position in this universe?							

Adopting Higher Ethical Standards

Road Signs	Yes	No	Status	The Next Point on the Path
Do I sometimes face conflicts between my attitudes or professional conducts and my personal moral values?	1 2 3	4 5		

APPENDIX I: MY CURRENT AND FUTURE POSITIONS

Road Signs	Yes	No	Status	The Next Point on the Path
Do I feel that I must sometimes ignore some unethical actions my boss or colleagues take, just for the sake of keeping things moving at work?	1 2 3	4 5		

THE BALANCED WAY

Road Signs	Yes			No		Status	The Next Point on the Path
Do I inform my colleagues that I do not accept unethical actions and that following a higher moral conduct should not hurt our company if our objectives are right?	1	2	3	4	5		

APPENDIX I: MY CURRENT AND FUTURE POSITIONS

Road Signs	Yes	No	Status	The Next Point on the Path
If my position in the company does not allow me to change its professional environment for the better, are there other opportunities for me to work in a different company?	1 2	3 4 5		

THE BALANCED WAY

Road Signs	Yes	No	Status	The Next Point on the Path
Do I have an "Ethical Tool Kit" that can guide me in making choices and decisions on matters not ethically clear to me?	1 2 3	4 5		

APPENDIX I: MY CURRENT AND FUTURE POSITIONS

Taking the Initiative

Road Signs	Yes			No	Status	The Next Point on the Path
Do I, every now and then, take time to reflect on my life, try to answer some nagging questions about how it is going, and think about ways to improve it?	1	2	3	4	5		

THE BALANCED WAY

Road Signs	Yes				No	Status	The Next Point on the Path
Can I, from this moment, specify things to do, on my own or with others, which can give me higher levels of excellence and contentment?	1	2	3	4	5		

Appendix II
My Personal Road Signs

Road Signs	Yes	No	Status	The Next Point on the Path
	1			
	2			
	3			
		4		
		5		

Appendix III

List of Quotations

"The best and safest thing is to keep a balance in your life, acknowledge the great powers around us and in us. If you can do that, and live that way, you are really a wise man," Euripides, 480 – 405 BC (keepingbalance.com).

"No student ever attains very eminent success by simply doing what is required of him: it is the amount and excellence of what is over and above the required, that determines the greatness of ultimate distinction," Charles Kendall Adams, 1835 – 1902 (brainyquote.com/quotes/quotes/c/charlesken197461.html).

"The toughest thing about success is that you've got to keep on being a success," Irving Berlin, 1888 – 1989. Quoted in *"The Merriam-Webster Dictionary of Quotations.* Springfield, MA: Merriam-Webster, Inc., Publishers, 1992, 402.

"I am going to let you in on a secret: You've already got everything you need to be happy." Stephen M. Pollan and

Mark Levine, *It's All in Your Head.* New York: HarperCollins Publishers, 2005, 1.

"Happiness consists in being happy with what we have got and with what we haven't got," Charles H. Spurgeon, 1834 –1892. Quoted in Bob Kelly, *Worth Repeating: More Than 5,000 Classic and Contemporary Quotes.* Grand Rapids, MI: Kregel Publications, 2003, 165.

"Content makes poor men rich; discontentment makes rich men poor," Benjamin Franklin, 1706–1790 (Quotationspage.com/quote/40270.html).

"I define joy as a sustained sense of well-being and internal peace - a connection to what matters," Oprah Winfrey (Quotationspage.com/quote/31099.html).

"We can be sure that the greatest hope for maintaining equilibrium in the face of any situation rests within ourselves," Francis J. Braceland, (Quotationspage.com/quote/33431.html).

"And heaven has He raised high, and He has set up the Balance; in order that ye may not transgress (due) balance," (*Qur'an* 55:7–8).

APPENDIX III: LIST OF QUOTATIONS

"So divinely is the world organized that every one of us, in our place and time, is in balance with everything else," Johann Wolfgang von Goethe, 1749 - 1832 (Quotationspage.com/quote/33430.html).

"The greatest discovery of my generation is that a human being can alter his life by altering his attitudes of mind," William James, 1842 – 1910 (Quotationspage.com/quote/1971.html).

"Happiness, misery, and instability come from within. It is we who give life its brightness or darkness, the same way the glass pot shapes the liquid inside it," Mohammad Al Ghazaly, 1917 – 1996. Qouted in Abullah Telmesani, *Between Acceptance and Excellence: Concepts and Principles on the Path to Success*. Jeddah, Saudi Arabia: Almahmoudiah, 2002, 13. (In Arabic language).

"I am as My servant expects from Me; if he expects good, he gets it; and if he expects bad, he gets it," (a *Divine Islamic Tradition (Hadith Qud'si)*).

"Don't curse time, for I am time," (a *Divine Islamic Tradition*).

"The only thing we have to fear is fear itself – nameless, unreasoning, unjustified terror which paralyses needed efforts to convert retreat into advance," Franklin D. Roosevelt, 1882 – 1945. Quoted in Robert I. Fitzhenry, ed., *The Harper Book of Quotations*. New York: HarperCollins Publications, 2005, 159.

"Only prayers can change destiny." (*Prophet Mohammed Traditions*).

"Verily never will God change the condition of people until they change what's in their hearts," (*Qur'an*, 13:11).

"Whatever missed you was not meant to hit you, and whatever hit you was inevitable (unavoidable)," (a *Prophet Mohammed Tradition*).

"We often ask, 'Why did you do that?'
or 'Why did I act like that?'
We do act, and yet everything we do
is God's creative action.
We look back and analyze the events of our lives,
but there is another way of seeing,
a backward-and-forward-at-once vision,
that is not rationally understandable.
Only God can understand it,"

APPENDIX III: LIST OF QUOTATIONS

Rumi, 1207 – 1273. Quoted in Coleman Barks, trans., *The Essential Rumi*. New York: HarperOne, 2004, 26–27.

"It really doesn't matter if the person who hurt you deserves to be forgiven. Forgiveness is a gift you give yourself. You have things to do and you want to move on." *Real Live Preacher* (Quotationspage.com/quote/31381.html).

"If you have made mistakes, even serious ones, there is always another chance for you. What we call failure is not the falling down, but the staying down," Mary Pickford, 1893 – 1979. Quoted in Applewood Books series, *Success: Quote/Unquote*. Bedford, Massachusetts: Applewood Books, Inc., 2002, 15.

"Without doubt, I am He that forgives again and again, those who repent, believe, do right, and are ready to receive true guidance," (*Qur'an*, 20:82).

"If one forgives and makes reconciliation, his reward is due from God: for He loveth not those who do wrong," (*Qur'an*, 42:40).

"Whoever is content will get contentment, and whoever is discontent (mad, furious, or rejecting) will get the same," (a *Divine Islamic Tradition*).

THE BALANCED WAY

"When you say "yes" to the "isness" of life, when you accept this moment as it is, you can feel a sense of spaciousness within you that is deeply peaceful." Eckhart Tolle, *Stillness Speaks*. Novato, California: New World Library, 2003, 67.

"Don't let your throat tighten with fear.
Take sips of breath all day and night,
before death closes your mouth,"
Rumi, 1207 – 1273. Quoted in Coleman Barks, trans., *The Essential Rumi*. New York: HarperOne, 2004, 52.

"I have learned from experience that the greater part of our happiness or misery depends upon our dispositions, and not upon our circumstances," Martha Washington, 1732 – 1802 (Quotationspage.com/quote/30517.html).

"Unrest of spirit is a mark of life; one problem after another presents itself and in the solving of them we can find our greatest pleasure," Karl Menninger, 1893 – 1990. Quoted in *The Merriam-Webster Dictionary of Quotations*, Springfield, MA: Merriam-Webster, Inc., Publishers, 1992, 340.

"He that is good for making excuses is seldom good for anything else," Benjamin Franklin, 1706 – 1790. Quoted

APPENDIX III: LIST OF QUOTATIONS

in Ashton Applewhite, William R. Evans III, and Andrew Frothingham, eds., *And I Quote: The Definitive Collection of Quotes, Sayings, and Jokes for the Contemporary Speechmakers.* New York: Thomas Dunne Books, 2003, 3.

"Nothing is particularly hard if you divide it into small jobs," Ray Kroc, 1862 – 1947. Quoted in Ashton Applewhite, William R. Evans III, and Andrew Frothingham, eds., *And I Quote: The Definitive Collection of Quotes, Sayings, and Jokes for the Contemporary Speechmakers.* New York: Thomas Dunne Books, 2003, 57.

"Whenever I hear, 'It can't be done,' I know I'm close to success," Michael Flatley (Quotationspage.com/quotes/Michael_Flatley).

"Frame every so-called disaster with these words…In five years, will this matter?" Regina Brett (cleveland.com/brett/blog/index.ssf/2006/05/regina_bretts_45_life_lessons.html).

"Many of life's failures are people who did not realize how close they were to success when they gave up," Thomas A. Edison, 1847 – 1931 (Quotationspage.com/quote/1977.html).

"I think the next best thing to solving a problem is finding some humor in it," Frank H. Clark, 1888 – 1962. Quoted in

Bob Kelly, *Worth Repeating: More Than 5,000 Classic and Contemporary Quotes*. Grand Rapids, MI: Kregel Publications, 2003, 284.

"Surely, there are obligations towards your Lord, other obligations towards yourself and still others towards your family, so you have to give each it's due," Salman Al Farisi. Quoted in Al Bukhari, *Sahih AlBukhari* 3:31:189.

"Ruined are the fanatics [who follow extremes in matters of Faith]," (a *Prophet Mohammed Tradition*).

"Every story has three sides to it – yours, mine and the facts," Foster Meharny Russell, 1864 – 1926 . Quoted in Robert I. Fitzhenry, ed., *The Harper Book of Quotations*. New York: HarperCollins Publications, 1993, 44.

"O you people, we have created you of man and woman and made you into nations and tribes so that you come to know one another. The most noble among you before God are the ones who are most righteous," (*Qur'an*, 49:13).

"Trust men and they will be true to you; treat them greatly and they will show themselves great," Ralph Waldo Emerson, 1803 – 1882. Quoted in *The Merriam-Webster Dictionary of Quotations*.

Springfield, MA: Merriam-Webster, Inc., Publishers, 1992, 424.

"He who mistrusts most should be trusted least," Theognis, 540 – 480 BC. Quoted in John M. Shanahan, *The Most Brilliant Thoughts of All Time.* New York: HarperCollins Publishers, Inc, 1999, 230.

"Respond in a better way; then will the one between whom and thee was enmity become as though he was a close friend," (*Qur'an,* 41: 34).

"When we fail, our pride supports us; when we succeed, it betrays us," Charles Caleb Colton, 1780 – 1832 (Quotationspage.com/quote/29067.html).

"Modesty is a shining light; it prepares the mind to receive knowledge, and the heart for truth," Madam Guizot, 1773 – 1827 (Quotationspage.com/quote/28907.html).

"Happiness is when what you think, what you say, and what you do are in harmony," Mahatma Gandhi, 1869 – 1948 (Quotationspage.com/quote/31095.html).

"We have indeed created man in the best form. Then we reduced him to the lowest of low. Except for those who believe and do righteous deeds: they shall receive endless reward," (*Qur'an* 95:4–6)

"Sin [unethical] is that which wavers in your heart and you do not want people to find out about it," Prophet Mohammed. Narrated by Muslim, *Sahih Muslim*. Riyadht, SA: Darussalam, 2007, 423.

"The beginning is the most important part of the work," Plato, 427 – 347 BC. Quoted in Ashton Applewhite, William R. Evans III, and Andrew Frothingham, eds., *And I Quote: The Definitive Collection of Quotes, Sayings, and Jokes for the Contemporary Speechmakers*. New York: Thomas Dunne Books, 2003, 24.

"The unexamined life is not worth living," Socrates, 469 – 399 BC (Quotationspage.com/quote/24198.html).

"Our repugnance to death increases in proportion to our consciousness of having lived in vain," William Hazlitt, 1778 – 1830. Quoted in John M. Shanahan, *The Most Brilliant Thoughts of all time* (New York: HarperCollins Publishers, Inc, 1999), 287.

Made in the USA
Lexington, KY
25 April 2010